POWER YOUR LIFE

WITH THE

Positive

Life Lessons and Secrets to Success from Luminaries and Everyday Heroes

CYRUS WEBB

Copyright © 2018 Cyrus Webb.

Published by Mango Publishing Group, a division of Mango Media Inc.

Cover and Layout Design: Elina Diaz

Mango is an active supporter of authors' rights to free speech and artistic expression in their books. The purpose of copyright is to encourage authors to produce exceptional works that enrich our culture and our open society.

Uploading or distributing photos, scans or any content from this book without prior permission is theft of the author's intellectual property. Please honor the author's work as you would your own. Thank you in advance for respecting our author's rights.

For permission requests, please contact the publisher at:

Mango Publishing Group
2850 Douglas Road, 3rd Floor
Coral Gables, FL 33134 USA
info@mango.bz

For special orders, quantity sales, course adoptions and corporate sales, please email the publisher at sales@mango.bz. For trade and wholesale sales, please contact Ingram Publisher Services at customer.service@ingramcontent.com or +1.800.509.4887.

Power Your Life with the Positive: Life Lessons and Secrets to Success from Luminaries and Everyday Heroes

Library of Congress Cataloging

ISBN: (print) 978-1-63353-748-4 (ebook) 978-1-63353-749-1
Library of Congress Control Number: 2018937910
BISAC category code: SEL027000 – SELF-HELP / Personal Growth / Success

To the Reader:

There are so many influences that can bring us down in life, making us feel as though nothing is possible and that our goals and dreams are unattainable. Maybe you find yourself surrounded by such negativity. Does it have to dictate what you are able to do in your own life? Absolutely not!

Through my radio show, magazine, and web series, I have interviewed over seventy-eight hundred guests from all walks of life. They might seem different at first glance, but each is a great example of someone who has accomplished amazing things while facing difficult circumstances. *Power Your Life with the Positive* draws on my interviews with forty such individuals, people who have overcome challenges, set goals, and exceeded them ... often bouncing back from difficulty to find their way to achievement.

But *Power Your Life with the Positive* does not end with the stories it tells—it continues with yours. After each profile, you will find questions and inspirational quotes to prompt thought, journaling, or discussion on what you have just read. To focus discussion and thought, as well as providing more "nugget-sized" inspiration, *Power Your Life with the Positive* includes "text-box" nuggets in each profile that you can draw on for yourself.

Nothing in life is impossible. Your goals and dreams are worth fighting for. Let these examples give you the fuel you need to power your life with the positive and leave the negativity behind.

—Cyrus Webb

TABLE OF CONTENTS

PROFILE #1:
GIVE YOURSELF PERMISSION TO FOCUS AND REFOCUS IN LIFE

Actress, Producer, and Author Robinne Lee

Robinne Lee is a talented producer, actress and author, a woman known for movies like *Deliver Us from Eva* and *Seven Pounds*, as well as the hit show on BET, *Being Mary Jane*. Her fans went crazy when she joined the cast of the *Fifty Shades* franchise, and she spends a lot of time promoting her work, which includes her new novel, *The Idea of You*. Her busy life shows how much effort Robinne has put into her work, but she is always eager to share with others how her success is something they can attain as well.

CW. Robinne, what has it been like for you to reflect on this amazing ride that you have had, not only as an actor and a producer, but now as an author?

RL. You know, I think I am the kind of person ... I am a little bit of a "Type A" person. I am very controlling, but I also don't like to sit still.

I feel like I need to be creating and evolving, and I think that it is important to keep finding things that feed your soul, your heart, and your brain.

And for me, I've always appreciated storytelling in any aspect, and I have always written for myself for joy since I was little. I just kind of did it for pleasure. And the same with acting—it has always given me pleasure, but acting is different in the fact in the way that you are waiting for someone to give you permission to act. You kind of have to rely on other people to support you.

Writing is something that I just sit down anywhere with my laptop and create and have something to show for it.

CW. That control is definitely a great thing. I think so many times, even in other professions, we give up so much of our power, and we wait on opportunities that in many ways and now especially with technology and the way that the world is that we can create for ourselves. People have gotten to know you over the years because of these amazing characters that you brought to life and dramas and comedies you've been a part of. Do you think that also helped set the stage for where you are now with books, where you are able to bring us a little bit of laughter and a little bit of drama but also, you know, those really deep personalities you have gotten to play and gotten to know yourself?

RL. Right! I think that it all feeds into each other. If you are a person and paying attention and living and breathing in the world, you hold onto these things. You hold onto these experiences and you hold on to all of the parts that make you who you are. At least as an artist I kind of store them up so I can use them in future projects, and whether or not it's something that I've borrowed from the behavior of one character or a voice or something, it's like having a treasure of materials that you can dip into. And so I think all of these little things that you do, everything you experience and the way you experience the world kind of really helps you as an artist, as long as you make yourself open to experiencing new things and you kind of walk around as if you don't have any skin and allow situations in different environments to affect you.

CW. Your main character in your book, *The Idea of You*, is having to definitely find her way as many of us do. There is so much we can learn from her experiences that play into what others can realize about powering their lives with the positive. Part of Celine, the main character of your book, is her ability to change and adapt when things weren't going well. What do you want readers to think about when they read Celine's words about realizing that you can redefine yourself and that you can really be whatever you really want to be?

RL. I felt, at twenty, like the choices that I made then were going to lead me on a path to a certain place, and that I wasn't going to be able to change direction. I wanted to try all of these different things, but I also had these fears that maybe I am not focusing enough. I did have friends who came out of college and then went straight to law school, and they were on a certain path. They then became law professors, etc. They were on this certain trajectory, but I feel like if you know what you want to do from the time you are young that's one thing, but if you don't know what you want to do you shouldn't feel like, "I've got to figure it out right now."

There is time to figure it out. And even if you do figure it out, you can re-figure it out and you can reinvent yourself. You are not running out of time.

I love that you can continue to redefine and you can continue to choose who you are and who you are going to be at any age until you die. Don't be afraid to make mistakes.

1. Have you started on the journey to doing what you love in life?

2. If it hasn't worked out, how can you redefine your goal for yourself and give it another shot?

Power Your Life WITH IMAGINATION

"Imagination will often carry us to worlds that never were. But without it we go nowhere."

—Carl Sagan

Power Your Life WITH FEARLESS PROGRESS

"Don't shortchange the future, because of fear in the present."

—Barack Obama

Power Your Life BY LETTING YOUR LIGHT SHINE

"Darkness cannot drive out darkness; only light can do that. Hate cannot drive out hate; only love can do that."

—Martin Luther King, Jr.

Power Your Life BY STANDING ON THE SHOULDERS OF GIANTS

"I am where I am because of the bridges that I crossed. Sojourner Truth was a bridge. Harriet Tubman was a bridge. Ida B. Wells was a bridge. Madame C. J. Walker was a bridge. Fannie Lou Hamer was a bridge."

—Oprah Winfrey

PROFILE #2:
ACKNOWLEDGE DOUBT,
BUT DON'T GIVE IN TO IT

Writer, Producer, and Author Paul T. Scheuring

When you say the name Paul Scheuring, the first thing that comes to the minds of many is his hit show *Prison Break*, but he has had a remarkable career as a writer and producer. In 2017, he added another title to his name, Amazon Top 100 Bestseller, with the debut of his first novel, *The Far Shore*. When we talked about his career and the journey to powering his own life with positivity and believing in himself and his abilities, it was obvious he had found his calling.

CW. Paul when you reflect on the life that you have been able to have and all that has come your way, do you think it is the result of your knowing what you were meant to do and staying true to that?

PS. I mean obviously as a screenwriter you often are a writer for hire and you have to write to what a studio or a network wants. You know there are certain projects, both in Hollywood and obviously personally with writing a book, where you write characters, and you know essentially who they are, when they start, and you have a fundamental idea of where you want them to go—but really it's a far more immersive process.

I think that's what keeps writers coming back. It is that process of discovery daily. If you allow yourself as a writer to just go, saying to yourself:

> *I don't know exactly what's going to happen here, but I am going to follow the moment and see what's real from the character.*

For the moment you know that's your calling and the reader discovers that as well.

CW. When did you know for you that this was a gift that you had, that this was something you were put here to do?

PS. You know, that's interesting. I think a lot of people look at it differently, and I am always suspect of people referring to their own gift, because:

> *I don't know that I have a gift—and I think that most creative people are full of doubt.*

But you have kind of this mission, this thing that it can really hurt to do ... and that is to creatively express yourself. It's filled with uncertainty and often you want to quit, but there is nothing else that you can do. There is nothing else that you can see yourself doing, and it becomes this kind of holy burden where you know this is the thing that I guess I am put here to do and develop how can I use that.

What's unfortunate is that so many people sit down to write a screenplay or a book or whatever, and they find out how excruciating it is, and then they quit after that one. And generally speaking, the first one is really just a foundation for the second, which in turn is the foundation for the third and the fourth and the fifth— and then all of sudden you've written ten or twenty or thirty, and now you are actually some version of a writer, and all of a sudden people are paying you, and there is a funny saying in Hollywood, which is: "Stick around for ten and we'll have to hire you, because the rest of the people quit."

CW. I'm glad you bring up the longevity, because I think that is so important to anything that we choose to do. I also want to ask you about the reward. Has that been one of the things that's been interesting for you along the way as to how you define success for yourself?

PS. Yes, absolutely. I came to realize very early on that success isn't measured by how much money you make or how many awards you win or people that you know. Or even, in this day and age, by how many tweets and how many likes you get and that kind of stuff. All that is totally hollow, because if that's the only wagon that you hitch your horse to, you are going to be empty. I am keeping my eye on the things that really matter. I think we as creative types can contribute to the world if somebody—and I do think there will be people out there—will read something we've done and say, "Wow, you know that makes me think differently. That makes me want to go out and explore and expand my boundaries and become something more than what I thought I could be."

If you are doing that as a writer or a singer or what have you, then you are adding value, because you know:

At the end of the day if the only reason that you are doing it is so that people will pat you on the back, you are going to be miserable.

But if you feel like you know at the end of the day you're making a difference, and you are on your deathbed and you can say, "You know what, a few people gained from what I did," then you can say it was worth it, and that's what I am hoping to do.

1. How can you evaluate what you are doing and how you might can be of service to others and not just make it about yourself?

2. Like Paul, is there a way to gauge how you can "power up" your life and make it more fulfilling by doing something that you truly love?

Power Your Life BY GIVING BACK

"Each of us has the potential to contribute. You have a great opportunity to make a new shape of the world."

—14th Dalai Lama

Power Your Life BY FOLLOWING THROUGH

"To accomplish great things we must not only act, but also dream; not only plan, but also believe."

—Anatole France

Power Your Life WITH HUMILITY

"I also am other than what I imagine myself to be. To know this is forgiveness."

—Simone Weil

Power Your Life WITH DARING

"Never be limited by other people's limited imaginations."

—Dr. Mae Jemison, first African-American female astronaut

PROFILE #3:
TAKE PLEASURE IN LEARNING

Actor, Producer, TV Personality, and Author LeVar Burton

Everyone knows him from *Roots*, but I have been a fan of LeVar Burton since I was a kid. Before he was a part of *Star Trek: The Next Generation*, he was the host of *Reading Rainbow*, the show that made me want to have a platform to encourage reading and meaningful conversations. To talk with him about life, his impact on others, and the possibilities for us all was not just inspiring, but something that I know will remind you that your life can have an impact on others.

CW. LeVar, you have been able to touch so many lives through your work, especially through the platform that is *Reading Rainbow*. What has it been like for you to use your life as an example as to what is possible?

LB. It has been truly remarkable. My mom was an English teacher, and she always had several books for her own personal pleasure.

Reading for me was like breathing. It is a natural part of the human experience.

All the work is because of the woman my mother is, and that has allowed me to humbly have the impact that I have.

CW. I can definitely agree with that. Part of the great thing is that books can connect us all and share life lessons that can change our lives. How you always understood that impact?

LV. You know I have! Some people say you are what you eat. I genuinely believe you are what you read. I am aware of how my life has been enhanced by being a lifelong reader. I genuinely believe that if you are literate in at least one language, you are my definition of free.

A lifelong reader has the ability to be a lifelong learner. If you are a learner for life then you are a dangerous individual, because you don't have to take anyone's word for anything. You can read and learn for yourself.

I know there is a link between that which we imagine and that which we manifest in this realm. It is the imagination that connects us all. It's also our imagination that connects us to our birthright that is storytelling.

1. Reading is like breathing for LeVar. What is the one thing that you feel as though you can't do without?

2. What makes you feel free, and how can you best use that to power your life in a positive way?

Power Your Life WITH FAMILY TRADITION

"For I am my mother's daughter, and the drums of Africa still beat in my heart."

—Mary McLeod Bethune

Power Your Life BY BEING OPEN TO DISCOVERY

"A good traveler has no fixed plans and is not intent upon arriving."

—Laozi

Power Your Life
BY GROWING TOWARDS FREEDOM

"I have observed this in my experience of slavery, that whenever my condition was improved, instead of increasing my contentment; it only increased my desire to be free, and set me thinking of plans to gain my freedom."

—Frederick Douglass

Power Your Life WITH THE POWER OF LOVE

"It is good to love many things, for therein lies the true strength, and whosoever loves much performs much, and can accomplish much, and what is done in love, is well done."

—Vincent van Gogh

PROFILE #4:
ACKNOWLEDGE THE CHALLENGE, HAVE FAITH, AND MOVE FORWARD

Actor, Writer, and Producer Jeryl Prescott

On January 10, 2017, one of the most talked-about movies of 2016 made its way into stores and digital outlets: *The Birth of a Nation*. Based on the true story of Nat Turner, the enslaved man who inspired many and led a rebellion against those who held sway over them, the film's talented cast included actress Jeryl Prescott, who has brought so many amazing characters to life over the years, including on the popular television show The Walking Dead on AMC and on BET's *Rebel*, as well as her own project called *Stand Down Soldier*.

I had a chance to sit down with Jeryl and discuss not just *The Birth of a Nation*, but also what it's been like for her to slip into the skin of various characters, sharing some amazing stories along the way and producing her own content.

"Every time I get a job as an actress, I consider it a small miracle," she told me. Her desire to act came from her roots in the church. "The church is where I learned to play the piano and find the confidence to speak in front of a crowd and take a bigger leadership role," she says. "That gave me the confidence and the interest in being on stage and having something to say. That's how I began to see myself as an actress."

She went to college and did theater, but even though she saw herself doing more, Jeryl experienced what so many do when it comes to pursuing their goals and dreams: the individuals who told her what wasn't going to be possible for her. "Nonetheless, I've been able to find a variety of roles to play," she says. Jeryl went further, touching on the many conversations taking place about the roles of women—and especially women of color—"It's suggestive of the need for diversity and an appreciation of diversity. We have always met challenges and worked to create spaces for ourselves."

"Every profession will offer certain challenges. You have to go into it with a positive attitude and the belief that God put you there for something and move forward."

Talking about *The Birth of a Nation*, Jeryl says, "It is a powerful project, and I am so grateful to Nate Parker. Nate Parker is an amazingly generous and bold director, producer, and writer. I have an amazing amount of anticipation about the journey of this film."

Jeryl's journey continues not only with exciting projects, but also with the relationships she is forging along the way. Whether discussing the talented cast of *The Birth of a Nation* or *The Walking Dead*, she says "There's an immortality that comes with all acting. The fans hold on to you and never let you go. The friendships that I developed have been real." Speaking of *The Walking Dead* in particular, she says this: "The show will never die, because it constantly asks us to search inside of ourselves. It's a constant universal questioning."

At the time of our conversation, Jeryl was gearing up for the release of a project, produced by her, that was on its way to television.

"You continue to pray, create, make connections, and speak it into reality as much as you can. It's wonderful when you see things actually materialized."

This is what she told me when referring to what happened in 2017. "If it's part of a larger plan for me it will happen."

1. How has what others say you can do affected how you approach your life and your dreams?

2. Like Jeryl, how can you change the way you look at where you are and where you want to go?

Power Your Life BY BELIEVING IN YOURSELF

> ## "Do not let the bastards grind you down."
>
> ### —Margaret Atwood

Power Your Life BY DEVELOPING AND GROWING

> ## "Life isn't about finding yourself. Life is about creating yourself."
>
> ### —George Bernard Shaw

Power Your Life BY SEIZING CONTROL

> ## "Freedom is never given; it is won."
>
> ### —A. Philip Randolph

Power Your Life WITH GRATITUDE

"We tend to forget that happiness doesn't come as a result of getting something we don't have, but rather of recognizing and appreciating what we do have."

—Frederick Koenig

PROFILE #5:
START WHERE YOU ARE AND DON'T GIVE UP

Producer and Author Peter Engel

I didn't know the name Peter Engel before 2016, but I think everyone knows *Saved by The Bell*. It was the television show that created stars and a brand that continues even today. Well, Peter Engel was the creator of that show and many others like it. When he released his memoir, *I Was Saved by The Bell*, it opened my eyes up to so much about his life and where he was today—and our conversation together was so encouraging for me and I know for you when it comes to the importance of having a positive attitude in life.

CW. Peter, first of all, I have to say that what you have built through your production company is truly inspiring. What has it been like for you to open up about your personal and professional journey the way you have?

PE. Cyrus, you said the important word: "journey." It has been a journey, and sharing it with people has been a great part of it. I hope it makes them feel like you can't give up.

> *I've had my heart broken so many times, but I've come to realize that if you didn't have your heart broken, the victory wouldn't be as sweet.*

CW. You really seem to have a way of bringing characters to life. You talk about in your book about how just by reading about them, people want to see your characters on the screen. Have you always known that was your gift?

PE. Yes! I knew it when I put on my first show. I knew then it was something within me. The problem is that sometimes it's hard to get a chance.

> *It's hard to get your foot in the door, but you just gotta go with it. You just gotta keep fighting. That doesn't mean I was all the way in. I just had my foot in the door, but that was a start. Just keep in mind that you can't give up. If you love it, and have a passion for it, you'll have to stay at it.*

CW. In your book, you make it very clear that your faith is something that has guided and directed you in life. How has the knowledge that you were created with greatness inside you affected the way you live your life?

PE. I have always believed I was created for greatness, but it didn't happen right away. God made this promise to me, but it didn't happen overnight. You have to have faith. That is the only thing that will keep you from leaning too much on yourself. If you think you don't have to have faith, you'll think you can do it alone.

People forget it's supposed to be fun. For me the work is fun, and if you can have fun doing your job you can't ask for more than that.

1. Do a self-check and ask whether, like Peter, the work you are doing is fun for you. If not, how can you change that around?

2. Faith is an important aspect to having a positive life. What do you have faith in, and how can that help you to change the way you see where you are and where you want to go?

Power Your Life WITH VISION

"Where there is no vision, there is no hope."

—George Washington Carver

Power Your Life BY LISTENING TO YOUR HEART

"It is only with the heart that one can see rightly; what is essential is invisible to the eye."

—Antoine de Saint Exupéry
(The Little Prince)

Power Your Life BY DOING WHAT YOU LOVE

"My Vocation is my Vacation. I love what I do."

—Nick Cannon

Power Your Life BY GETTING BACK UP AGAIN

"The road back may not be as short as we wish ... but there are solid reasons to feel confident about the future."

—Richard Parsons

PROFILE #6:
RECOGNIZE THE POWER OF YOUR GIFT

Singer and Actress Antonique Smith

Recording artist and actress Antonique Smith is on a high like you wouldn't believe—and she is enjoying every minute of it.

Her first single, "Hold Up Wait a Minute," was nominated for a Grammy in 2015, and people around the world are talking about her emergence on the musical scene, especially after the release of her project *Love Is Everything*. Before "Hold Up," many knew Antonique as a Broadway star and as an actress who played Faith Evans in the hit movie *Notorious*, but music has always been a part of who she is. In 2017, she also was a part of the powerful limited television series called *Shots Fired*.

I asked Antonique what the ride of her journey has been like. "I'm so grateful," she told me. "I've been dreaming about this moment since I was a little girl. I'm so grateful that everybody is supporting and embracing it."

Though she has always believed in herself, Antonique told me that the competitive nature of the industry wore her down a bit. "Through the years, after seeing how difficult the industry is, I lost some of the belief I had in myself because of the rejection and the No's." She then added: "The majority of what you get are the No's. The tiny Yes's you get are what people normally see." She says it's been a long road, but her family, friends and fans have all made it worthwhile.

With the challenges of the industry, I was curious as to where the tenacity she has comes from. "I believe that my gift was an answer to a prayer of seven-year old Antonique," she told me.

> *"I think that God gave me something to share with the world. That is what keeps me going. This is the only thing I have wanted to do."*

Talking about the live performance, she says "That's my favorite thing. I love looking into people's eyes and feeling what they are feeling. To have that connection with people is priceless."

And this is only the beginning for her. "I'm going to keep going until I can't go any more," she says. "I continue to push."

1. For Antonique having some success is not enough. She keeps pushing. What can you do to keep pushing towards your goals?

2. The right attitude has helped Antonique to keep the right perspective. How can you change your attitude to better approach your own life and what you want to do?

Power Your Life BY SHOWING UP

"Face front, true believer!"

—Stan Lee

Power Your Life WITH YOUR UNIQUENESS

"There is a vitality, a life force, an energy, a quickening that is translated through you into action, and because there is only one of you in all of time, this expression is unique. And if you block it, it will never exist through any other medium and it will be lost."

—Martha Graham

Power Your Life BY RISING TO THE CHALLENGE

"Nothing, I am sure, calls forth the faculties so much as the being obliged to struggle with the world."

—Mary Wollstonecraft

Power Your Life WITH HOPE

"[N]o human being can truly be imprisoned if hope burns in your heart."

—Barack Obama

PROFILE #7:
YOUR GIFT IS BIGGER THAN YOU

Actor, Choreographer, and Author

Darrin Dewitt Henson

Whether it is movies like *Stomp the Yard*, television shows like *Soul Food*, or books like *Pregnant with Thought*, Darrin Dewitt Henson has been able to gives audiences around the world something that they can connect to—and there is no sign of him slowing down. His new book, *Ain't That the Truth*, released at the end of 2017, allows us to see so much about the inner resources he has used to get to where he is, and why it is so important for him to share his vision of inner growth with others.

We've had several opportunities to connect in conversations that are inspiring and uplifting, and this discussion about the importance of powering life with the positive didn't disappoint.

CW. Darrin, you have been fortunate enough to have a career that you and others love, but you have also used your platform to reach others. Why has that been important for you to do?

DH. I believe the platform is not just for me. It's to afford people the opportunity to be inspired, so they can be able to move on and do something for their lives as well.

For any of us, when you receive something, it's not just for you, but for you to share with others.

CW. Have you always known that the creative process was the way you would reach the world?

DH. I have! Creativity is my form of communication. Communication when it comes to the arts, like everything else, is consistently evolving. That has given me a variety of ways that I can communicate: acting, dancing, speaking, writing, etc.

There are so many ways we can expand. I'm just using some of those tools right now in my life.

CW. One of the things you have talked about is purpose. I believe that one thing that keeps people from walking in their purpose is fear. How have you not allowed fear to stop you?

DH. I do get fearful, but I use fear against itself. Some fear is good fear, stopping you from doing things that are detrimental. When it's fear of growing we know it's not good. You have to go through fear to get to where you want to be. Sit down, write down and figure out what you desire in life. In order for you to get there you'll have to go through fear. There is no other way.

> *If you understand that everything you want is on the other side of fear, you'll understand why stopping is not an option. Be scared but do it anyway.*

CW. I mentioned that the world has gotten to know you, in one way or another, through the way you communicate. When you hear the response to your work, is that validation that you are accomplishing what you want?

DH. Yes I do. Especially when it comes to my books. I want to remind people that they are bigger and better than they appear to be. I want to remind people that doubt kills more dreams than anything else, and never doubt what they can achieve. If they are willing to do the work anything is possible.

1. What is the way you communicate to the world, and what can you use from Darrin's approach to help you do it more?

2. How can you change the way fear is keeping you from living a positive and more productive life?

Power Your Life BY MAKING A DECISION

"I have learned over the years that when one's mind is made up, this diminishes fear."

—Rosa Parks

Power Your Life BY REACHING OUT

"Fear makes strangers of people who should be friends."

—Shirley McClaine

Power Your Life BY FINDING YOUR HAPPINESS

"Don't wait around for other people to be happy for you. Any happiness you get, you've got to make yourself."

—Alice Walker

Power Your Life WITH A SENSE OF WONDER

"There are two ways to live your life. One is as though nothing is a miracle. The other is as though everything is a miracle."

—Albert Einstein

PROFILE #8:
SHINE A LIGHT ON WHAT MAKES YOU SPECIAL

Actor, Producer, and Recording Artist
John Schneider

Whether you recognize him as Bo Duke from *The Dukes of Hazzard* or the infamous Jim Cryer from Tyler Perry's *The Haves and the Have Nots*, John Schneider has made name for himself, not just in television and movies, but in music as well. Over the last few years, he has been able to explore another arena, that of being a writer and producer, with his 2014 horror film *Smothered* getting rave reviews.

We talked about his career, his passion, and how he has stayed true to himself along the way.

CW. John, it is a true honor to speak with you for this. You have had such an amazing career in front of the camera and on stage. What has it been like for you to bring the characters you have to life?

JS. It's been fantastic. I am so delighted to be have been around long enough to do what it is that I love and to have someone recognize my work.

> *I think that we all have different parts in us. As an actor, you have a chance to shine a light on a particular trait, and to have people respond to that is amazing.*

CW. Did you always know that acting was the gift, that you were put here to do?

JS. Absolutely. I went from watching movies when I was very little to being in my first play when I was eight years old. I wanted to be on stage, wanted to be on camera ... wanted to have people eat popcorn watching me, and I never really strayed from that.

> *We are designed to do something. I think what I see more times than not is probably what you were designed to do is not something others understand. Hopefully your friends and life don't talk you out of it.*

There is nothing more depressing to me than seeing someone who is not in pursuit of their dream. It's better to be pursuing something that you're passionate about than spending your life doing something that you're not.

1. Have you, like John, realized early on that there was something that you wanted to do in your life? Have others supported you or discouraged you?

2. How can you hear and learn from the message that you were given something that was meant to be shared with others? What do you want to share with others?

Power Your Life BY DEVELOPING YOUR OWN IDENTITY

"If we stop defining each other by what we are not and start defining ourselves by who we are—we can all be freer."

—Emma Watson

Power Your Life WITH CURIOSITY

"The important thing is not to stop questioning. Curiosity has its own reason for existence."

—Albert Einstein

Power Your Life WITH CONFIDENCE

"If you're presenting yourself with confidence, you can pull off pretty much anything."

—Katy Perry

Power Your Life BY NOT FORCING IT

"If only we'd stop trying to be happy we could have a pretty good time."

—Edith Wharton

PROFILE #9:
BE CONFIDENT, EVEN ON THE BAD DAYS

Supermodel and Author Tess Holliday

Supermodel Tess Holiday first got on my radar because of her inspiring (and oftentimes funny) messages online, but when I discovered she was from my home state of Mississippi, I became even more intrigued with her, because she was yet another example of what was possible for anyone with a dream. I didn't know much about her backstory, however, until she released her memoir in 2017, called *The Not So Subtle Art of Being A Fat Girl*. In it, she chronicles not just her success as a plus-size model, but lets the world into her struggles and challenges growing up in a book that is sure to inspire people around the world.

"Growing up down South, I resented it for a long time," Tess told me during our conversation together after the book's release. "I felt like people didn't understand me. I never told anyone I was from Mississippi. I think I was angry for all of the wrong reasons." Now she uses where she is from as a mirror for others. "Just because you have had a bad experience doesn't mean that where you're from is bad," she shares.

"You can go anywhere in the world and feel bad. Traveling all over I see that I could have had it way worse. I'm really grateful for my experiences and the opportunity to look back on them."

Discussing her no-nonsense approach to life, Tess says her honesty is part of what her fans expect from her. "My fans are from all walks of life, all over the world. Some don't even know what I'm saying because of language barriers. They do understand that it's hard to grow up in certain areas and be different. I know a lot of people identify with me because they feel alone."

"Life can be hard, but if you have people who support and love you it can also be really great."

She also realizes that just because she is so outspoken doesn't mean everything is perfect. "I think it's important to tell people that just because I wrote a book about confidence doesn't mean that I always love myself and that I don't have bad days. I try to be as honest as possible. I know what it's like to not feel great all the time. I'm really glad to be on the other side and to understand that it's ok to have those days. It doesn't make me a bad person. It makes me human."

And now that she has graced magazines and runways around the world, what does Tess want? Well, everything! "I've accomplished everything I set out to do, and now I find myself coming up with more dreams and seeing what's next." If the past is any indication, then the sky's certainly the limit for her.

1. How can you use negativity to power your desire to continue pursuing your passion?

2. Who can you surround yourself with (either in person, online, or through books) that motivates and pushes you forward?

Power Your Life WITH GOOD PEOPLE

"Surround yourself with people who take their work seriously, but not themselves, those who work hard and play hard."

—Colin Powell

Power Your Life WITH POSITIVE THOUGHTS

"A man is but the product of his thoughts. What he thinks, he becomes."

—Ghandi

Power Your Life BY DEFYING EXPECTATIONS

"There is nothing a woman can't do. Men might think they do things all by themselves but a woman is always there guiding them or helping them."

—Marjorie Joyner

Power Your Life BY CHOOSING GOOD CHEER

"For every minute you are angry you lose sixty seconds of happiness."

—Ralph Waldo Emerson

PROFILE #10:
SHARE YOUR STORY AND CHANGE THE WORLD

Fitness Model, Trainer, and Photographer

Wendell B.

We all need to have examples around us of individuals who have set goals, met them, and inspire others to do the same. One of those people for me has been Wendell B. He is a fitness model, trainer, photographer, and an example that life is all about what you choose to do with it.

He has been an example to people around the world as to what is possible—and the passion he has for his work is amazing to me. He's been a repeat guest on the radio show *Conversations LIVE*, and in this conversation we talked about his commitment to himself, his audience, the importance of association and why it is imperative that you take care of yourself along the way.

CW. Wendell, glad to have a chance to talk with you again. One of the things that we share in common is our love of positivity and being able to inspire and motivate people.

WB. That's one of the things that drew me to you in the beginning, and it has been great to kind of follow that journey that you've been on. What has that been like for you when you kind of reflect on it, especially these past couple of years, to be able to do what you love but then to be able to motivate people along the way?

I wasn't expecting it, because I've never been that type of person at first to just to be, "Oh I am going to motivate the world."

It all started for me just wanting to better myself and be a better me. And just by me sharing my story and being transparent, it just helped others in the process.

I am thankful that just me being myself I have been able to help others all just stemming from me basically want to help myself and hold myself accountable. I am truly grateful for the platform and Instagram for being there to help me be that voice to help other people to get through their situation.

CW. You are right. I mean Instagram is definitely that place for you. At the time that we are having this conversation, over thirty-seven thousand have joined you there on Instagram. Do you still have those wow moments when you kind of think about that?

WB. Yes, actually I am still wowed sometimes, because it's really intriguing to know that so many people find me this interesting, like my page, and want to follow my daily life to see what I am posting and to see what I am just doing on a daily basis. It's kind of insane for me, because like I said it all started just for being me, so when I go places and I see people and they know who I am, they sometimes kind of catch me off-guard because I am still a regular person. It's a great feeling … I can't lie. It's a great feeling just to hear somebody telling me that you impact them in a positive way, it's not just, "Oh, you have all of these types of followers and all of these people and you are not doing nothing with it." So I am just grateful to know that I am touching people in that way.

CW. One of the things that you shared at the end of December of 2017 was your best nine pictures that got the most attention. I mean of course, you know, you have gotten hundreds of thousands of likes on these pictures. We talked last year about how a lot of people wait until January to kind of get things started, and how one of the big pieces of advice that you gave was taking advantage of now. You shared in one of those pictures, which got a lot of attention, how you'd had some moments when you had not been, you know, as committed, and that you have kind of gone back a little bit. What was it like for you, for one to be able to share that to let us know that, but then to know how you are bouncing back?

WB. The response that I got from that post was wild. I had actually sent the picture to a friend of mine who is actually one of my business partners with me and I told her I was kind of embarrassed to post the picture, because people look at me as, "Okay, you are getting these results—you are behind the product, and you know you are supposed to have these great results." She reminded me that at the beginning you promised yourself and you promised everybody that you will always be real, and you will always be transparent, and you will always just share your story. So to have so many likes and so much feedback from me just being transparent and seeing my downfall, it made me feel so much better, because it made me realize ...

What I am doing is really helping people. This is my purpose. This is what I am supposed to do. My falling off wasn't just a bad thing for me. It was actually a good thing for me because I was able to get results and show people how to get results.

It took me falling off, but now I can recommit a whole new amount of people that haven't seen my journey from the beginning. They can see me now work on my results from this point that I am at now. This is my way to let them know that it's not just that you get results and you keep them. You have to work at it. None of us are perfect. Everyone has their ways and everyone will fall off. And I just want to be that voice for people to let you know that everyone is normal. Every day is not going to be a good day. You are going to fall off, but the thing about it is you have to be able to pick yourself up and just know how to keep going no matter what.

CW. I want to stay with that for a moment, Wendell, because you mentioned in that post two things: One of course has to do with eating. Which, I mean ... we *all* can relate to that. The second thing you mentioned caused you trouble was not being consistent, and that ties into what you just said, because I think a lot of the time, and this is just in life in general, I think that we all get to a place where we do get comfortable and think, "Okay, I have done this, so I am good." I mean, do you find that pictures like that post and the response keep you moving and not being complacent?

WB. Actually, it really does—because when I originally started my journey, as I always said, I posted my first post on Instagram. That's how I was able to grow that following, and feeling like this and being transparent is my way of keeping myself accountable.

I had no friends to hold me accountable at the time; no one wanted to work out with me or eat clean with me. So my response to that was to post all of these pictures of what I was unhappy with, just so I could see myself daily and know what I needed to change.

So for a while I kind of fell out of that mindset, because I had then got to a point where I kind of plateaued. And at that point in my mindset, it's like, "I can help others," but at the same time I kind of forgot about myself. And you have to find time, in between doing everything that you are doing, to not forget about yourself. You have to focus on yourself, because if you are not helping yourself, how are you going to help someone else?

CW. Wendell, you have done so much as a fitness model and trainer—but there are still other things you have also been able to achieve, especially with photography. To be an entrepreneur is another thing that a lot of people are experiencing this year. What has that part of the experience been like for you, to be able to have started this business and to let us know about it on Instagram, so you can build it through Instagram and share it with us that way?

WB. I shocked myself, honestly, at the way that my photography business has grown in a short period of time, and it's only going to grow from here. From when I was a child, I always knew that I wanted to be my own boss. I wanted to be an entrepreneur, but I never knew what it was going to be that I ended up doing. And even through a couple of years ago I used to always be down and out, not having extra money for things, and I just talked to my mother and say I wish I had other things that I could do to earn extra money. She always told me it will eventually come to you. Just be patient. And it's so ironic how this can tie into my Herbalife experience (which is what Wendell has used along his weight loss and fitness journey). Herbalife is not about just the weight loss. It's about the Mental Health, and like I said before, it took me going to an event to hear what the speakers said you have to do.

I started reflecting on my childhood and things that you enjoy doing as a child. With me, I always enjoyed taking pictures as a child. Never knew that I could build a business out of it. I just did it for fun. So when I got the experience, and I was able to invest in a camera, I started playing around with it at first and didn't think about it still as a business until people started motivating me and telling me that my work was good. They told me to keep going. I was able to grow a photography business in just ten months, just on something that I enjoy doing!

CW. Got you, and in that same vein as we were talking about motivating yourself along with the tribe, you know one of the things that we've all heard—and I am a firm believer in—is that leaders are definitely readers. You have been talking about that, even in your post on Instagram. I want to broaden that a little bit, and not just talk about what you are reading, but also the people that you associated with. This is a really good point, because I think again this is one thing that we have in common, Wendell. Talk to us about how important it's been for you to be able to make sure that you are watching those around you—but also you talk about this in your post, as well as about encouraging your audience to keep the negativity away. How has that helped you in meeting your goals?

WB.

It's very, very important to watch who you are around. It might sound cliché, but it's very true when people say that you are what hang around.

And when you really paying attention to it, if you are hanging around people that just want to do drugs or just want to go out and party all the time, nine times out of ten you're going to be doing the same thing. So why not hang with people that are reading books, people that want to start businesses and do positive things and are always encouraging you to do positive things?

> *If you hang around positivity, you will become the positive. I always tell myself I want to be the least smart in the group that I am in, because I am always looking to learn and grow more. I don't want to be the smartest one, because how am I going to grow?*

Always challenge yourself to just be around new people. I have lost so many friends over the years, and it's not a bad thing that sometimes you just outgrow people. God puts them in your life for a reason, and you just have to move forward to new levels and new people that are put in your life that are going to take you to a different level and be more positive.

1. Who in your life can you lean on to hold you accountable for your attitude and your dreams?

2. What are some things you would like to do that maybe you have held off on pursuing?

Power Your Life WITH DISCOVERY

"Somewhere, something incredible is waiting to be known."

—Carl Sagan

Power Your Life BY SETTING BOUNDARIES

"You can and should set your own limits and clearly articulate them. This takes courage, but it is also liberating and empowering, and often earns you new respect."

—Rosalind Brewer

Power Your Life WITH AUTHENTICITY

"Never apologize for showing feeling, my friend. Remember that when you do so, you apologize for truth."

—Benjamin Disraeli

Power Your Life BY INSPIRING OTHERS

"I have this ability to find this hidden talent in people that sometimes even they didn't know they had."

—Berry Gordy

PROFILE #11:
STAND IN YOUR POWER

Singer and Actor Willie Taylor

Music lovers around the world first got to know Willie Taylor with the formation of the R&B group *Day 26* in August 2007, but the music that was burning inside of him began long before the reality show that introduced him and the group. It was something that was always meant to come out. Since that time, he has found success not just with his musical brothers, but with his solo career and even as an actor on stage and on television.

Over the past few years, I have interviewed Willie several times. One thing that has always struck me was his ability to not only think for himself but make the case for his career better than anyone else could. At a time when popular music is not always good music, he has managed to give his fans a combination of both.

Willie Taylor on the Love of His Fans: "It is still amazing to me, how they have always been there, from *Day 26* to now, when I am doing my own thing. They are the people who keep me going. Just to know that they rock with me means a lot. It just feels great to have their support."

Willie Taylor on His Solo Career: "This is my time to let you know exactly who I am as an individual.

> *When you listen to my music, I want you to be able to say, 'I know exactly where he's at. I understand.' It's my way of being able to make a clean slate and let my words and talent speak for me.*

I'm a fan of my music first. I expect everyone else will love it the way I do."

Willie Taylor on What Keeps Him Going: "I have so much more to give. Yes, I'm completely excited about the success I have had up to this point, and I could have stopped ... but that's not me. When I do stop, I want to have really made my mark on music. When I am long gone, I want people to be singing my music and remember who I am.

> *The truth is I can't stop until I give them (my fans) all that I got. I have an insane work ethic and an incredible drive. I never see myself failing, so I never fail. It's like I really believe I'm going to win.*

Once that's in my mind, I don't do anything that won't allow me to win. I always see myself winning."

Willie Taylor on the Gift: "I want people to know the gift. I am a true believer in God, and I'm a true artist."

"My work ethic will outdo my talent any day. I'm a talented individual, but I work so hard. That's why I am not going to stop."

"I'm a believer in myself, and I want you all to believe in me as well. I'm a well-rounded artist and business man. I want to be a household name. I want you to say that the name Willie Taylor means something. That's what I'm working towards."

No matter what he does musically, moving forward Willie Taylor is definitely going to be making his mark on the industry. As his star continues to rise, he gives this advice for others: "I want you to stay true to yourself. Don't feel like you have to follow the trends. Remember you have to love it first. When you love it your audience will love it. Most of all, trust in God and work hard. Make sure you put your all into it."

1. Ask yourself: Could you like Willie do what you love even if no one else believed in you?

2. What can you do to look at life more positively, even through the challenges you face?

Power Your Life WITH PURPOSE

"To rank the effort above the prize may be called love."

—Confucius

Power Your Life BY USING THE MAGIC INSIDE YOU

"We do not need magic to transform our world. We carry all the power we need inside ourselves already. We have the power to imagine better."

—J.K. Rowling

Power Your Life BY BUCKING THE TREND

"History has always been a series of pendulum swings, but the individual doesn't have to get caught in that."

—Robert L. Johnson

Power Your Life BY BEING YOURSELF

"Defining myself, as opposed to being defined by others, is one of the most difficult challenges I face."

—Carol Moseley Braun

PROFILE #12:
CONSISTENCY IS THE KEY TO LONGEVITY

Singer Johnny Gill

Timeless. That is just one way to describe Grammy-nominated recording artist Johnny Gill. With the recent BET mini-series on the group *New Edition*, there has been renewed appreciation for what artists like him bring to the table. Many have gotten to know him for his hit singles, like "My, My, My," "Rub You the Right Way" and "Where Do We Go from Here" (with Stacy Lattisaw), as well as his involvement with the popular groups New Edition and LSG ... however, there seems to be no substitute for the man himself.

With his last full-length album, *Game Changer*, Johnny Gill fed his fans' insatiable appetite for new music. And has been traveling the world, feeling the love around the way.

"I have been blessed with a gift from God that is magical. You can't design it," Johnny told me in our conversation together.

> *"I think about my career and how my music has touched people. It is beyond a miracle and a blessing. To have people to connect with you is a gift."*

Like many other soulful singers before him, Johnny Gill began singing in the church and blossomed from there. He believes the main reason he is still able to do what he loves is because he understands the importance of staying consistent. "I stay true to me and my music," he says. "If you look at my body of work you'll see that I'm open to trying new things.

> *At the end of the day my biggest goal is to always stay focused and be careful that I don't lose who I am.*

I set out to make great music, songs I can identify with and connect with, and do it justice." Remaining true has given him the confidence to say that in spite of it all, he has put his heart and soul into each and every project. "I have something to hold my head up about and be proud," he says. That comes from walking in his musical truth.

His beginnings were not so full of pride. Johnny relayed to me how when he first started in the business at the age of fifteen, he was not always the best of himself. "There was no blueprint about how you are supposed to be and act," he told me. "All the things you have to learn growing up in this business— the ups and downs that come with it—now make me blessed that I have my fans there for support." He understands that it is all a process, a machine that brings it all to life. The process that gets his music to the masses is something he feels more connected with, and he knows it's important not to take any of it lightly. That is what keeps him going. That is what makes him a winner.

1. What can you do to keep from losing your way while trying to power your life with the positive?

2. Johnny was able to reflect on what he's done in his life and use that as motivation. What have you done that brings you pride and encourages you to keep going?

Power Your Life BY BELIEVING IN YOURSELF

"Belief in oneself and knowing who you are, I mean, that's the foundation for everything great."

—Jay-Z

Power Your Life WITH CONFIDENCE

"[I]f one advances confidently in the direction of his dreams, and endeavors to live the life which he has imagined, he will meet with a success unexpected in common hours."

—Henry David Thoreau

Power Your Life WITH YOUR HEART

"The best and most beautiful things in the world cannot be seen nor even touched, but just felt in the heart."

—Anne Sullivan
(teacher of Helen Keller)

Power Your Life WITH CONTAGIOUS LAUGHTER

"Count your age by friends, not years. Count your life by smiles, not tears."

—John Lennon

PROFILE #13:
BLAZE A TRAIL. LIGHT THE WAY.

Singer Keith Sweat

After three decades in the music business, on Tuesday, January 17, 2017, R&B legend Keith Sweat began a new chapter in his award-winning career: a residency at the Flamingo Hotel & Casino in Las Vegas. The singer who has brought the world great songs like "Make It Last Forever," "Twisted," "How Deep Is Your Love," and "Nobody" was able to spend time with his fans, sharing music that they have come to enjoy.

"I helped a lot of people grow in terms of their relationships and growing up with me musically," he told me. "A lot of people don't get that opportunity."

Powerful stories and videos have also come along with the songs that he has released, narratives that seem to connect with the listener, bringing them into each verse. Keith says it's easy for him to do the videos because "I have it in my mind when I'm in the studio."

Outside of releasing music, Keith Sweat has also taken to the airwaves as a radio personality and made a name for himself as an author of a book about relationships. All of this has been eagerly welcomed by his male and female fans. "I can't really say I'm the doctor of love," he told me with a laugh. What he does say is that he tries to let his audience know that when it comes to relationships "it takes time and it take understanding, because no two people are the same." He also adds, "Every relationship takes work and needs work," and both parties have to be willing to do the work necessary for it to last.

Along with helping others appreciate what it takes to make a relationship last, as he celebrates his thirtieth anniversary in a competitive industry, Keith is showing other artists what it takes to have longevity. "It's great to be the godfather for other artists," he told him. Talking about those who have been inspired by him, he says that his experience shows other artists that they can have just as long of a career.

"The key to it all is to stay ahead and do as well as you can musically."

"For me to open doors for other artists and them to appreciate that means a lot," he says.

Regarding his Vegas residency, Keith has called it the "second act" of his career. When asked to elaborate on that, he told me this: "I've done everything else. When you're going into a whole new arena, it creates another journey. Going into Vegas for the first time in the residency is like going to Broadway. It's a new step in my career. It's a new platform that I have to step on."

> *"I've learned a long time ago that anything worth having is worth working for."*

"I'm hoping this is something that my fans will be glad I have done."

1. Is there something you haven't tried that, like Keith, you are willing to give a shot, even though you don't know how it will turn out?

2. Keith alluded to the key to longevity being staying ahead over time. How can you best use your time to get the outcome you want in life?

Power Your Life WITH SELF-LIBERATION

"The cost of liberty is less than the price of repression."

—W. E. B. Du Bois

Power Your Life WITH GRIT

"Never give in, never give in, never, never, never, never—in nothing, great or small, large or petty—never give in except to convictions of honor and good sense."

—Winston Churchill

Power Your Life BY BEING AN EXPLORER

"The world is full of wonderful things you haven't seen yet. Don't ever give up on the chance of seeing them."

—J.K. Rowling

Power Your Life WITH KINDNESS

"Always be a little kinder than necessary."

—J.M. Barrie

PROFILE #14:
TAKE ADVANTAGE OF A SECOND CHANCE

Media Personality and Author Rolonda Watts

Like many people around the world, I have been a fan of Rolonda Watts for quite some time. What she has accomplished as a journalist and media personality has definitely set her apart from others, and in 2016 she added the title of Author to her already impressive resume, publishing the novel *Destiny Lingers*.

Her book is one of those books that reaches you wherever you might be and reminds us of what is still possible. "*Destiny Lingers* has been a life journey for me," Rolonda told me during the discussion.

> *"I have to admit that it started off as a hobby. I would go to the beach with my friends. They brought a book to read. I brought a book to write. ... I had so much I wanted to say that I determined myself to turn it into a novel."*

At the core of the book are questions about the main characters Destiny and Chase that we, as readers, can ask ourselves when it comes to our lives:

"What if two individuals who couldn't be together had a chance to meet again? What would you do with the second chance at your first love?"

"I'm not Destiny," Rolonda tells me when I asked her what it was like to slip into the character's skin and tell this story. "When I writing the story, it was painful for me. I'm a lot more ballsy a woman (than Destiny). It was so interesting, having a relationship with her during this journey. Destiny is like a lot of girls, more methodical, more thoughtful. Destiny is more in her head. ... She's so available to love and doesn't know where to find it." She finds such love, however, in Chase.

The story mirrors life today for so many. There are those who are raised a certain way, with certain beliefs. Will their children and their children's children continue with that way of thinking or choose another path? Discussing her generation and those who have come up since, Rolanda says this: "We have the choice to make that difference." And that is exactly what she has chosen to do and wants others to do as well.

1. What from your past might be keeping you from pursuing your true love?

2. In Rolonda's book, *Destiny Lingers*, the characters get a second chance at love. How can you start today, taking advantage of the opportunity to start over in a more positive direction in your life?

Power Your Life BY APPRECIATING WHERE YOU'VE BEEN

"All that happens to us, including our humiliations, our misfortunes, our embarrassments, all is given to us as raw material, as clay, so that we may shape our art."

—Jorge Luis Borges

Power Your Life BY OVERCOMING

"[A]lthough the world is full of suffering, it is full also of the overcoming of it."

—Helen Keller

Power Your Life WITH GRIT

"Change depends on persistence. Change requires determination."

—Barack Obama

PROFILE #15:
LET YOUR LOVE MOTIVATE YOU

Actor Bruno Gunn

At the suggestion of a friend, Bruno Gunn decided to take an acting class, and two decades later he has never looked back.

He's appeared on acclaimed television shows over the years, like *Sons of Anarchy* and *Westworld*, as well as movies like *The Hunger Games* and more.

> **Life has been good to him, but it has not come without hard work, dedication, sacrifices, and faith.**

I connected with him via social media and invited him to chat with me about his journey. He graciously accepted, and the conversation that followed is sure to inspire you.

"It's an exciting time," Gunn told me, referring to his career and the projects he's been able to do. "I'm blessed and fortunate to be a part of it."

I was curious how he had been able to balance the work he's done and the success that has come his way. "So many times you get caught up in it," he told me. "You want to be present for all of it. Sometimes things are up, sometimes things are down. You [can] forget to take the time to look back and see how far you've come and what you've accomplished." Realizing the importance of it, though, he added:

> *"It's always great to reflect on where you've been and the work you've done. It gives you the confidence in your gut—you know this is what you're supposed to do."*

If individuals are looking at the entertainment industry and life in front of the cameras as a get-rich-quick opportunity, Gunn says that is not what you're going to get. "You don't become an actor because it's a good financial decision," he says. "You become an actor because you are passionate about the work. You love the work. I always let that motivation push me. I'm not going to quit."

Gunn is convinced that the perspective he has is what helps him to stay grounded.

"You can't get caught up in what's happening," he says. "You just have to focus on the work. I've got faith and confidence in the work. I've turned it over to something bigger than me. I'm a storyteller. Telling stories is what we do."

Part of the fun he told is being able to slip into the skin of various characters across his career and see the way others respond. "Fans have embraced me," he says. "How wonderful it is to have such a group rooting for you." A large part of that group comes from social media. "I'm a big fan of social media," he told me, which again is how we initially connected. "It's an amazing tool to connect with people across the world in real-time. That's some power. I've made some great friends via social media."

Part of the connection that Bruno Gunn believes his fans feel is his desire to get to know each character that he portrays. "Every character has pain," he told me. Even in the greatest moment there's still pain. I'm always striving to find what is my character's pain. I let that be the moral compass as to where [the character] goes."

Knowing that he is giving his best is one thing, but realizing that others are inspired by him takes Gunn's appreciation to another level.

> *"You're doing more than collecting a paycheck. You're moving people's lives. You're helping them find some direction or giving them hope. We all need hope. Hope is what keeps us going."*

"If someone can gather a little hope from something I did, that's a beautiful thing."

1. Bruno has been able to overcome challenges in pursuit of what he loves. How can you better do the same in pursuing what you want to achieve?

2. Social media is just one way to connect. How can you use that platform to connect with like-minded individuals who can inspire and motivate you?

Power Your Life WITH SELF-ACCEPTANCE

"Self-love has very little to do with how you feel about your outer self. It's about accepting all of yourself."

—Tyra Banks

Power Your Life WITH CARING

"Taking care of yourself makes you stronger for everyone in your life … including you."

—Kelly Rudolph

Power Your Life BY KEEPING YOUR EYES OPEN

"Let your hook always be cast; in the pool where you least expect it, there will be fish."

—Ovid

Power Your Life BY ACCEPTING GOOD DAYS AND BAD

"Life is like this: sometimes sun, sometimes rain."

—Fijian proverb

PROFILE #16:
DON'T BE AFRAID TO ACT

Actress and Author Tina Alexis Allen

All of us have the ability to make a difference, and Tina Alexis Allen is using her platform in the public to do just that. As a playwright, actress, and now author (her memoir, *Hiding Out*, went on sale in February 2018), she is using her public profile to raise awareness for causes that matter to her and having fun along the way. Her breakout role since 2016 has been as Shurn on the hit show on WGN called *Outsiders*.

At the beginning of 2016, she tweeted this:

> *"Stop looking around for permission to do or be anything. Just act into it."*

Those words seem to be guiding her path, too.

I asked her how she was able to gain the boldness and courage it takes to do what you love and stay consistent with it. "I think I've always been a risk-taker," she told me. "I'm a big believer of doing whatever you want at any age. I just feel like we are so capable as human beings. ... Most of us don't know how much energy and ability is within us."

Talking about her home life and the optimism she has, Allen added: "I come from a place of "everything is possible"—you just have to get up and do it, and not look for permission."

Being in an industry where there is so much competition, Allen says that she feels like a "blessed gal" to be a part of a cast and show like *Outsiders*. She told me ...

"Getting a job where I can work with people who are fantastic human beings and actors [is an amazing feeling]."

"There is something about the work that has always been at the core of what I love. It's the intimacy of interacting with other human beings on such high stakes and creating this magical world."

I asked her whether it was a surprise to see how people have taken to the show. "I knew it was a great show," Allen says, adding, "One can never tell how the public perception will be." Part of what she feels as possibly driving the success is the fact that her work is "touching on some important messages like what it means to be an outsider." While filming the show, she told me that she thought "there's going to be a big group of people that will relate."

Outside of television and plays, Allen is also building a brand that includes a jewellery line, taking something that can be deadly—an actual bullet—and transforming it into something beautiful. She says that she hopes others are able to realize that no matter where they are in their lives or what their profession, they can make a difference, too.

"I think the key that I've learned through this process is that we can start at any time," she told me. "We're here to help each other and love each other. That's really what feels the most satisfying."

1. Pushing the reset on your life right now, what can you do to move in a positive direction?

2. Regardless of what others might say, is living a life pursuing your passion worth it to you?

Power Your Life BY GETTING BACK

"The greatest glory in living lies not in never falling, but in rising every time we fall."

—Nelson Mandela

Power Your Life BY PERSEVERING

"Keep going. No matter what."

—Reginald Lewis

Power Your Life WITH PASSION

"Passion is energy. Feel the power that comes from focusing on what excites you."

—Oprah Winfrey

Power Your Life WITH FORGIVENESS

"To err is human, to forgive divine."

—Alexander Pope

PROFILE #17:
ADAPT AS YOUR WORLD CHANGES

Comedian and Actor Jamie Kennedy

Jamie Kennedy is one of those actors that you have been able to see on a variety of both television programs as well as movies. I remember watching him now almost twenty years ago when he first appeared on screen, but many of you of course got to know him because of *Malibu's Most Wanted* and other movies like *Romeo and Juliet*. More recently he's been seen in diverse projects like the film *Buddy Hutchins*.

It was actually the film *Buddy Hutchins* that brought us together for the first time. We talked about that project, his career, and what tools he is using to continue to connect with his fans around the world.

CW. Jamie, the landscape of the entertainment industry has changed a lot since you first came on the scene. What has it been like for you to navigate those changes?

JK. You know this new world, it moves so quick and so fast and things do change very quickly. It's been interesting.

CW. It also says a lot about you as well that you have been able to not only do projects that people talk about, but also that you have been able to stay consistent along the way. What do you think has been the key for you to be able to stay consistent and stay relevant in this business?

JK.

You have got to adapt or die. Before all the time it would just be doing movies, movies. And then it's like movies and TV. Now it's movies, TV and digital projects. You have to do everything.

I believe it's not just about me making something and you watching it. It's almost like you've got to be a part of it.

Everything in our world is transparent, so I think as long as you move with the times you'll be okay.

CW. That brings us to your fans, Jamie. Is that something that you've gotten more comfortable with, knowing you have this base that will follow you wherever you go?

JK. I love it, and I am very fortunate that people have liked me and will follow me. If it wasn't for them I wouldn't have my house or, you know, I wouldn't be able to eat—so they have been the conduit to make my dreams come true.

> *I try to do things that I like and then I try to do things that I think other people will like so hopefully you know our tastes are aligned.*

CW. Jamie what keeps it fun for you? What is it that keeps you excited about acting?

JK. Well I'm excited about the art of acting. It's great when you get something really great and well written and you can act out. Let's say you do a movie, right, and you do the movie and you've made these choices—and then you don't know if they are working or not until, like, nine months later until you have a screening of it. And when you see that people connected with what you did … that's fun, you know?

> *The reason I am doing this stuff is because I kind of have to or else I would go crazy. It's who I am.*

I have these like intuitions, and I want to share them with you—and I need an outlet. And so what's really great is when people say, "Hey man, that was funny" or "Yo, I like that character." It's kind of like cleansing your soul—that's what I think creating is. It's like I wanted to get that out, and then if somebody likes it along with you then that feels good.

1. Jamie recognized the need to adapt in order to keep moving forward. How can you do the same when it comes to what you want to achieve?

2. What keeps your goal or dream fun—and are you spending time finding ways to do more of that?

Power Your Life BY PREPARING FOR CHANGE

"One of the challenges associated with a company becoming large is that companies become hierarchical. They become bureaucratic. They become slow. They become risk averse."

—Kenneth C. Frazier

Power Your Life BY TAKING JOY IN LIFE

"I have found that if you love life, life will love you back."

—Arthur Rubinstein

Power Your Life WITH SELF-LOVE

"You yourself, as much as anybody in the entire universe, deserve your love and affection."

—Buddha

Power Your Life WITH APPRECIATION

"One's life has value so long as one attributes value to the life of others, by means of love, friendship, indignation, and compassion."

—Simone de Beauvoir

PROFILE #18:
DON'T DESPISE SMALL BEGINNINGS

Recording Artist Ruben Studdard

Talking with platinum-selling recording artist and *American Idol* winner Ruben Studdard has, without a doubt, been inspiring for me personally. Both of us coming from the South, I responded to his humility and appreciation for where he came from, but also where he found himself today.

He was in the middle of a whirlwind schedule of performances and press, but was very gracious with his time. In this conversation he discusses the road to stardom, what keeps him grounded, and ultimately what it means for him to be a great artist.

Ruben on the Musical Platform: "I just wanted to sing. After you try so much, you really just want to be heard. When I finally made it on *American Idol*, I wanted people to hear me and enjoy me. To be an inspiration is really a blessing. I most definitely can attest to what perseverance can do for you."

Ruben on Responsibility as as Artist:

> *"My responsibility lies with my relationship with God. I wanted to make sure that I made music with integrity."*

"The music I make is something that I could sit in a room with my grandmother and listen to with no regrets."

Ruben on Fans After *Idol*: "It was awesome. You never really get to see or feel what is going on outside of the show. When I got home for the first time and to have people waiting on me at the airport was a shock. We as artists would be nothing without them."

Ruben on Comparisons to Luther: "It was pressure in the beginning because I never considered myself in that category. I have always put Luther on a pedestal. It was kinda heavy because it's a lot of expectation. Some expect you to produce that kind of high quality music. I now believe it's more about what you make them feel rather than my actually singing like him. That's a compliment."

Ruben on Being Himself: "Your first album you don't have as much say-so as you might feel like you should. You have to go with the flow. Clive Davis helped to maneuver me through my first album. The older I get and the more creative control I have, I am able to do more of my own thing and have a lot more say-so. This allows me to show people who I am. I just want to be myself and sing."

Ruben on Separating His Personal Life from His Professional Life:

"I felt in the beginning it was important to separate the two. When you listen to all the greats, though, the further they get in their career they become more transparent. That resonates with their fans."

"Being so private isn't as important as you think it is. It's good to keep your business to yourself, but the only way you can sing songs that really matter to people is if you've actually gone through stuff."

"I can't act like my life is perfect. It's unfair to believe that people never go through things. I go through stuff, and I'm able to move on."

Ruben on Success: "For me now, success is longevity. A lot of times people feel that every time out is not going to be just the highs. You have to sustain yourself through the highs and lows if you want to make it in this business, or in any business."

1. How has where you come from influenced you?

2. With Ruben as an example, is it possible for you to move past a difficult situation and focus on what is still possible for you in the future?

Power Your Life BY STAYING TRUE TO YOUR ROOTS

"Change your opinions, keep to your principles; change your leaves, keep intact your roots."

—Victor Hugo

Power Your Life BY LOOKING TOWARDS THE FUTURE

"When one door of happiness closes, another opens; but often we look so long at the closed door that we do not see the one which has been opened for us."

—Helen Keller

Power Your Life WITH POSSIBILITY

> "Once you choose hope,
> anything's possible."

> —Christopher Reeve

**Power Your Life BY BEING A HELP,
INCLUDING TO YOURSELF**

> "Two things stand like stone: kindness in
> another's trouble, courage in your own."

> —Princess Diana

PROFILE #19:
LEARN FROM OTHERS, BUT BE YOURSELF

Author, Actress, and Producer Omegia Keeys

I've gotten to know bestselling author, writer, actress, and producer Omegia Keeys over the past seven years, and one thing is for certain:

She is someone who plays by her own rules.

Before 2017, it had been two years since the two of us had seen each other in person, but during her visit to Mississippi—taping segments for her new docu-series *From Jim to James Crow*—we had a chance to talk about the amazing journey she has been on since the last time we met. That included everything from acting in television shows and movies to producing her own content and even writing *The Brown Girls Guide to Good Credit*, a book on personal financial management.

The first question that came to mind when we began the conversation was about where the courage comes from to do all that she does. "From my mom and my great-auntie," she answered quickly. They taught her to "do it, because they couldn't. They instilled in me to don't let anyone tell me no." Omegia then adds, "I've been that way ever since I was young."

One of the highlights for her company, AboutFace Media, has been the web series *Donors*, something that Omegia says was not planned. "The web series was never supposed to be," she told me. "I was going to jump straight up into the feature." Having her credentials as a filmmaker questioned, however, led her to take out her frustration in words. "I wrote the first episode overnight because someone ticked me off," she explained.

"My writing ability when I'm mad or upset comes out so crystal clear."

"I got to do this wonderful backstory that served as preparation for the feature."

In 2017, she released a book to help with building and maintaining credit and announced her newest project, the docu-series called *From Jim to James Crow*, which looks at the institution of racism throughout the country over the years. She was inspired by the discussion around football player Colin Kaepernik I even had the privilege to narrate that project—a first for me as well. Omegia debuted *From Jim to James Crow* in Atlanta, Georgia, on February 25, 2018.

No matter whether she is writing a novel or screenplay, acting, or directing, Omegia Keeys says that the written word is her gift. "And who am I not to follow this gift," she asks.

1. What is the gift that you feel like you have been given that you can't let go of?

2. Even if you are experiencing setbacks or delays, how can you stay positive about what you are doing?

Power Your Life WITH CREATIVITY

"You can't use up creativity. The more you use, the more you have."

—Maya Angelou

Power Your Life WITH DARING

"Life is either a daring adventure or nothing. To keep our faces toward change and behave like free spirits in the presence of fate is strength undefeatable."

—Helen Keller

Power Your Life BY BEING YOUR OWN FRIEND

"Before we can make friends with anyone else, we must first make friends with ourselves."

—Eleanor Roosevelt

Power Your Life BY SURVIVING

"In three words I can sum up everything I've learned about life—It goes on."

—Robert Frost

PROFILE #20:
OWN THE RESPONSIBILITY YOU'VE BEEN GIVEN

Actor, Writer, and Director Philip K. Boyd

Ever since he was five years old, Philip K. Boyd knew he wanted to entertain. Now as an actor, writer, and director he is able to do just that, and the world is able to come along for the ride. For twenty years, he has been working hard, honing his craft and seeing it all come together over time in the television shows and movies he's been able to be a part of. Recently, millions around the world were introduced to his character Oscar on the hit show written, directed, and produced by Tyler Perry called *The Haves and the Have Nots*.

Though he stays constantly on the go, Boyd says about his career:

"I look back on it and say I have been able to live my dream and do things I wanted to do in my life."

What a great thing to reflect on! When it comes to acting, he says, "Being able to create anything in life is what it's all about. Being an actor and being able to be different characters is very fulfilling for me."

At a young age, he knew he wanted to "be a lot of different things" in his life. He says that this inspiration influenced him to "create different personalities and characters" and set the stage for where he is today.

His career as a working actor is not something that Boyd takes lightly. "It creates a level of responsibility that you have to own," he says. "When you're creating characters you want to give the fans what they want."

> *That sense of responsibility is also part of the gratitude that he has.*

"Anytime I get a phone call that I've booked a job it makes you want to work harder and be better than you were before. I'm still climbing up the ladder."

> *"It's about constantly working, constantly creating and trying to be better and make it to the next level."*

Being a part of the successful series *The Haves and the Have Nots* is definitely part of that next level. "Tyler Perry is a very special person," Boyd says. "He is a great storyteller. He has an energy about him that is infectious. The people that are surrounded by him make it their own personal journey to be better. I feel honored and blessed to be a part of this show, and to be around the amount of talent that is on it."

For fans of the show, part of the fun of Oscar's character has been watching how he continues to evolve. "I kinda had an idea of where the character was going throughout the show," he told me. Outside of *The Haves and the Have Nots*, Boyd says he just wants to be able to use his life and path as an example for others.

"If I can inspire one person in the world to chase their dream, then I feel as though my job is done."

1. Looking at Philip, how can you continue to make what you do fun?

2. Just as the character Oscar has evolved, how can you evolve and grow, entering a more positive place?

Power Your Life WITH BRAVERY

"We are going on swinging bravely forward along the grand high road and already behind the distant mountains is the promise of the sun."

—Winston Churchill

Power Your Life BY REALIZING YOUR POTENTIAL

"With realization of one's own potential and self-confidence in one's ability, one can build a better world."

—14th Dalai Lama

Power Your Life BY CHOOSING TO ACT

"The most difficult thing is the decision to act. The rest is merely tenacity. The fears are paper tigers. You can do anything you decide to do."

—Amelia Earhart

Power Your Life BY TAKING A CHANCE

"I want to stop transforming and just start being."

—Ursula Burns

PROFILE #21:
A SETBACK IS A RESET, NOT THE END

Fitness Trainer and Model Branden Nicholson

Have you identified your "why?" The question might seem strange to some, but it is one that each of us has to consider, no matter where we are in life.

> *Every day we make decisions about things that we do or don't do.*

These decisions then affect not only ourselves but also those around us. How many of us have seen something and said, "I want that," or, "I wish I could do that!" The obvious question to ask is, "Why?" The answer will determine if we are willing to do the work necessary to get what we say we want.

Fitness model and trainer Branden Nicholson has not only identified his "why," but found a personal motivation that literally affects each and every aspect of his life. Today he is positively impacting the lives of individuals around the world through his coaching and motivational tips, but the journey began with himself and the question of "why."

Nicholson, who is the founder and CEO of B. Nick Fitness, has dedicated his life not just to getting his clients in the best shape possible, but stimulating them mentally to face the challenges in front of them. His own love of fitness and wellness came eight years ago, when he snapped his right femur bone in half.

"I was rushed to the hospital and had three major surgeries that left me with a twenty-eight-inch rod in me, with four screws to hold it in place," he says.

> *"I was in the hospital for over two months. I could not walk for a full year."*

During this time, Nicholson went through that dark valley of doubt that so plagues so many. "I went from people and coaches calling me every day to everyone giving up on me, including the doctors. I was told I would never return to the football field and would never be able to walk again in life."

Some would have allowed that diagnosis to end any hope they had. Not Branden Nicholson.

> *"Through all of this, God was showing and telling me that this is not where I was going to end up at. I used my pain to push me through prosperity. I beat all odds against me."*

"I am here to tell you that when you are going through pain, I know exactly what you are feeling—because I have been there. I will tell you this much: if you work through your pain, the other side is your reward. I learned that pain isn't permanent. You can get through this, because you are bigger and better than your pain. I proved everyone wrong that tried to stop me—kill my dreams to walk again—that impossible is nothing."

> *"I got this far using my pain. God showed me he had a bigger plan for my life."*

That plan has included the work that B. Nick Fitness is doing through in-person training and online. "There's nothing like this," says Nicholson. "Through social media, I'm helping people that I can't reach change their lives by getting in shape and motivating them to get on the right track and stay there."

This is when the "why" is so important. "What keeps me motivated is knowing that I have people looking up to me. My clients and family look to me for support and assurance. My whole personal experience also motivates me." He also realizes the importance of focusing on what is important. Though many are impressed by physical appearance, Nicholson says that you can't be defined by what people see. "That comes and goes," he explains.

"You can look healthy on the outside and be crappy on the inside. It has to start within. That is your base. If the base isn't grounded it all falls apart. You have to stay focused and grounded. It's all about discipline."

Through the pictures of his clients that he shares online, we know that the approach that Branden Nicholson uses is paying off in the lives of others. "That's the best feeling in the world," he told me. "Even when I was playing ball, I never felt like this. Just to be a part of someone's life is big. When I get the chance to see them, that's a thrill for me."

"I came into this industry saying that if I can change one life, then this is the job for me. It's all about progression and taking one step at a time. All the lives I continue to change I give all the glory to God."

Nicholson has this message for anyone going through a trial or situation where they feel there is no hope: "I'm telling you not to give up but to push through it. Pain is temporary. It may last for a minute, hour, day or even a year, but eventually it will subside and something else would take its place. But if you quit that will last forever!"

1. Have you discovered your "why" in life?

2. How can you push past the pain and the negativity in life to stay true to your "why?"

Power Your Life WITH GOOD CHOICES

"Our deeds determine us, as much as we determine our deeds."

—George Eliot

Power Your Life WITH PERSEVERANCE

"You have only to go right on, and at the end of the road, be it short or long, victory and honor will be found."

—Winston Churchill

Power Your Life WITH PERSPECTIVE

"There are years that ask questions and years that answer."

—Zora Neale Hurston

Power Your Life WITH ENERGY

"It's my experience that folks who have no vices have generally very few virtues."

—Abraham Lincoln

PROFILE #22:
CREATE YOUR OWN LANE

Actor and Producer Chris Greene

Life has been good for actor and producer Chris Greene. He has been able to find his voice in front of the camera and bring the best of himself to a variety of characters in television shows like *Sleepy Hollow*, *Satisfaction*, *Complications*, *Being Mary Jane*, and the movie *Birth of a Nation*.

"I've been very fortunate," Greene says when reflecting on his work. "It is a struggle just like any other career, but at the end of the day it's been a great outlet for me."

> *"Something about acting—getting to imitate everyday life—is the most gratifying thing."*

"Being able to bring what I have been able to observe has been fantastic. It's the greatest job in the world."

When did he first realize acting was something he wanted to do? Greene says the seed was planted early. "My father collected movies. The movie that got me excited about acting was *Independence Day* (with Will

Smith). To see how his presence was on the screen made me say I want to affect people like that. From that point it was like, let me look into acting and see what it was all about." Green said that it all came together for him at the youthful age of nineteen when he was an extra on set.

"Once I got on an actual set, I was like, 'This is what I want to do with the rest of my life.' "

And that seed has been flourishing ever since.

When it comes to seeing the response to his work from fans, Greene says that it's "a little odd, but not in a bad way. It takes a little getting used to, but it's also very flattering to know that people are influenced by what you are doing. Your goal as an actor is to set out and tell a certain story and portray a certain being—when the people get it, it's gratifying." This has served the actor/director well when it comes to being a part of a wide variety of projects. "Part of this business is that you get cast off of how you look," he says. "I think as an actor my goal is to accept your type and go in and show people I'm not just this guy."

"I'm an actor. I feel like I can play everything to the best of my ability. It's good to be well-rounded because life is well-rounded."

Considering some of the productions he has been a part of—and the success of shows like *Complications*—some folks might expect Greene to be more "Hollywood" than he is. But he hasn't let fame go to his head, and he credits his ability to take it all in stride to his family and friends.

"My focus has been to keep that small circle around me that was there in the beginning," he explains.

"It keeps you from wanting to mimic anyone else." His being a father, it seems, is the greatest role he has snagged over the years—and it has affected him the most. "My daughter has saved my life in every sense," he says. "I was told when you have a child it is going to change you. She is everything. She has become my motivation. She's allowed me to look at stuff differently."

That might also explain why his idea of what success is has evolved over the years.

"Starting out it was more about being famous. Now for me it is about inspiring other people and having them enjoy my art and my passion. That, in turn, helps me enjoy the job even more."

Greene says it means a lot to him to know that he affected someone in a positive way and that he can leave something behind for future generations to be inspired by—including his daughter.

It is clear that Chris Greene has gotten to where he is because he hasn't been afraid to take chances.

It is something else which, like his love of movies, he got from his father. He says that his dad told him that you don't want to be on your deathbed and talk about the things you wanted to do instead of the things you had done. This has helped him to keep a balanced view of fear in mind. "My outlook on fear is totally different," he says. "I've found that for me fear is more of a motivator. When I get scared it makes me want to do it more just to not feel that way."

"I know that if I don't take the step to get past the fear I'm going to always go to the edge and not look over. Eventually you have to at least look over."

"For me, fear can be motivating or crippling, and I don't want to be crippled by the possibility of what if."

Greene says he tries to encourage others to surround themselves with individuals that will push you and encourage you to use your own passion. If you can do that, he says, fear will be more of an obstacle you go over instead of a roadblock.

1. What has been a motivator for you, and how can you better use that during the difficult times you might meet along your path?

2. Can you change your outlook on fear, like Chris has, and rush forward towards the thing that might scare you?

Power Your Life BY PUTTING YOURSELF OUT THERE

"The more one does and sees and feels, the more one is able to do, and the more genuine may be one's appreciation of fundamental things like home, and love, and understanding companionship."

—Amelia Earhart

Power Your Life WITH COURAGE

"One isn't necessarily born with courage, but one is born with potential. Without courage, we cannot practice any other virtue with consistency. We can't be kind, true, merciful, generous, or honest."

—Maya Angelou

Power Your Life WITH HOPE

"Nature has fixed no limits on our hopes."

—Björk

Power Your Life WITH SMILES

"I've got nothing to do today but smile."

—Paul Simon

PROFILE #23:
HONESTY GUIDES YOU TOWARDS SUCCESS

Actor, Producer, and Actor Dan Bucatinsky

For Dan Bucatinsky, living life authentically has paid off in a big way. He's an Emmy Award-winning actor (bringing to life James Novak on the hit ABC drama *Scandal*), writer, producer, and author—and he has done it all on his own terms. This doesn't mean that every day and every event he has experienced has been the best, but it does mean that he has not allowed the challenges he has faced to stop him.

As I chatted with Dan, it was clear why so many were inspired by him.

He's a man who is married to the love of his life, raising children and doing the kind of work that fulfills him.

When it comes to *Scandal*, it is the show's writing and Dan's portrayal of James that has been an inspiration to so many.

Just by living his life and doing what he loves, he has caused others to believe the same is possible for them.

Dan told me that knowing he has had that effect on others is "so fulfilling," and that sharing inspiration is what he hopes he can to do through his platform in the public.

The third season of *Scandal* saw the demise of Dan's character James, but the show and he have definitely made their mark on the world. I asked him if he was surprised by the response to the show and the way it continues to gain momentum. "In this day and age there is so much competition coming out of our computers and DVRs that anything that stands out in the clutter is a surprise," he told me. "I remember when I read the pilot of *Scandal*, I felt like Shonda had kind of reinvented the genre of the one-hour drama with that pilot. On the one hand, it is always a surprise when anything cuts through but, knowing Shonda and how talented she is and how innovative she is, I'm not surprised." Dan went on to say that he felt she had "changed our appetite for the speed and the complexity of storytelling, and other shows are trying to keep up."

Since his time on *Scandal* officially came to an end, Dan has been keeping busy on other projects, including the movie *The Post* starring Meryl Streep and Tom Hanks—and is showing no signs of slowing down. His advice for others when it comes to pursuing their dreams?

"I feel like the most important thing is to not give up."

He enjoys hiking and using his experience when tackling a steep hill. He shares this: "I know that if I stop, I definitely will never get to the top. As hard as it seems at times, we never really know what will happen unless we keep going. I ask myself, 'What are the other options?' I could move a little slower. I could take a little break, but I definitely don't want to ever stop."

May we remember that when we are facing our own steep hills in life.

1. What would help you to live life in a more authentic way?

2. Using Dan's analogy of climbing a hill, how can you vow to keep going when things look bleak in your life?

Power Your Life WITH COURAGE

"One isn't necessarily born with courage, but one is born with potential. Without courage, we cannot practice any other virtue with consistency. We can't be kind, true, merciful, generous, or honest."

—Maya Angelou

Power Your Life WITH VISION

"Have a vision. Be demanding."

—Colin Powell

Power Your Life WITH HONESTY

"You will make all kinds of mistakes; but as long as you are generous and true, and also fierce, you cannot hurt the world or even seriously distress her."

—Winston Churchill

Power Your Life BY TRYING AND IMPROVING

"If everything was perfect, you would never learn and you would never grow."

—Beyoncé Knowles

PROFILE #24:
BE WILLING TO MAKE OTHERS UNCOMFORTABLE

Actor, Producer, and Advocate Michael Cory Davis

When it comes to examples of individuals who know what they want in life and are going after it, you have to give a nod to actor and activist Michael Cory Davis.

Known to some for his roles on shows like the soap opera *All My Children* or on the Syfy network, Davis has gained international attention and respect because of the causes to which he has lent his time, energy and resources.

Never one to shy away from a challenge or an opportunity to provoke discussion, Davis stripped down for his 2011 calendar *Body of Change* as a way to raise awareness and funds for his nonprofit, Artists United for Social Justice. I have a great deal of respect for him, not just because of the way he conducts himself professionally, but also because of the way he uses the gift that is the public eye to make a difference.

In 2013, he launched his new campaign "I Stop Traffic," in an effort to increase awareness about child trafficking and the exploitation of American children by creating and distributing cause-related multimedia. In my conversation with him, Michael Davis discussed when he discovered his love of the arts, how he has chosen to use his celebrity when it comes to helping others, and even how he views what he has been able to achieve— and how can you can embrace your own power.

CW. Michael, when did you realize that you were interested in being in the entertainment industry?

MCD. My parents encouraged creativity. I was involved in a lot of school plays. Growing up I also got involved in debate school. I realized early on that I always had a flair for being on stage.

CW. Looking at what you have done so far and the projects you have been a part of, what surprises you the most about your career and how you are perceived?

MCD.

> *What continues to surprise me is that people are surprised that I am a black man that has taken on what has been seen as a woman's cause.*

Let's face it, when it comes to topics like human trafficking, it tends to be more Caucasians bringing attention to it. It never ceases to amaze me how people perceive me. I welcome the surprise, because I am able to turn over the perceptions and let the world see black men are more than what pop culture says we are.

I, as an independent filmmaker, have been able to do so much. I have been able to raise tens of thousands of dollars for orphanages in a country, Bulgaria, where I don't even speak the language.

My accomplishments let me know there is a whole lot more that we as artists can do to change the world in a positive way because we have the microphone to do it.

CW. You mentioned your work in Bulgaria. That is, in fact, how I first became aware of you because of your short film. For those who haven't seen it, *Svetlanta's Journey* is a film you wrote, directed, and produced that came about because of a victim of trafficking you met. She was a thirteen-year old Bulgarian girl who had basically been sold by her adoptive parents into prostitution. From meeting her, the project has gone on to not only win awards but aired on national television in Bulgaria. What did you take away from that project, regarding how we in the United States view issues like human trafficking and child prostitution?

MCD. I would say how ambivalent we sometimes are. If people are looking at children as commodities, that's a problem. If we have a society that has been victimized because they are not getting the services they need to heal, that's a problem. People don't speak enough about it, especially in the black community. I think that's why more haven't taken on the cause. At the end of the day it deals with a form of slavery, and we should know about it and care about it. I do understand, though, that a lot of the apathy about the subject is because a lot of us are so focused on our own problems.

CW. Michael, you are in a business that is covered from all angles, both the good and the bad. What are your thoughts about the twenty-four-hour news cycle and the public's desire to know so much about celebrities?

MCD. What's happened in society today is that we have made the Internet a loaded gun. People learn things and share things instantly. What's worse is that you have people who make money off what goes wrong in an individual's life. I don't know why it is that whenever someone is on top and doing well, there is some need for us to wait for that person to do something wrong.

When people look at me, I want them to know that I am just as human as they are. I am fully aware of the issues that we as men have with women.

> *Though I have my faults as a man, I have empathy and compassion towards women that are victimized and that's why I do what I do.*

CW. Michael, success is something that is relative to most people. What does success look like to you?

MCD.

> *Success, for me, is being able to overcome challenges without having to compromise myself and staying true to my authenticity.*

It's having the power to create my own content and not having to have my hand out in order to do so. Success is also when I am able to fulfill my purpose being on the planet, challenging myself and using my art and talent to move us all forward. That's not to say I'm always trying to do deep movies and stuff like that.

> *I just want to do what I love and help others in society along the way. That's when I am most happy. That's success.*

1. Like Michael, are there ways you can use your life for something bigger than yourself?

2. As you have been on your own journey, how has your idea of success changed?

Power Your Life WITH
THE POWER OF PERSPECTIVE

"Success is to be measured not so much by the position that one has reached in life as by the obstacles which he has overcome while trying to succeed."

—Booker T. Washington

Power Your Life BY APPRECIATING
YOUR HISTORY

"For Africa to me ... is more than a glamorous fact. It is a historical truth. No man can know where he is going unless he knows exactly where he has been and exactly how he arrived at his present place."

—Maya Angelou

Power Your Life WITH CARING

"You really can change the world if you care enough."

—Marian Wright Edelman

Power Your Life WITH KINDNESS

"Shall we make a new rule of life from tonight: always to try to be a little kinder than is necessary?"

—J.M. Barrie

PROFILE #25:
IF YOU STAY TRUE TO YOURSELF, OTHERS WILL RESPOND

Singer Jason Pure

Anyone who stays connected with recording artist Jason on social media has seen him using the hashtag #flyhigh. It was not just part of his promotional campaign for the single "Icarus," but a larger reminder for all of us.

If you haven't heard the single, I definitely encourage you to give it a listen. It shares the reminder to go as high as you can when it comes to your goals and dreams. That message is something Jason has been living and sharing with others. "It's been amazing," he told me when discussing the response to the single. "As with most musicians, I put in a lot of work into this song." He added, "It's definitely a message I was hoping would connect with people. That's all you want."

Making an impact is key part of what drives him. "My goal as an artist is to leave something that is long-lasting," he says.

It goes back to his personal connection with music as a listener. As an artist, Jason "wanted to be able to do the same for other people." That includes being able to "relay messages that would help other people."

At a time when everyone has an opinion about everything, sending a positive message through the static is not always easy to accomplish. I asked Jason where his confidence has come from. "That is a constant battle to get to that point," he admitted. "It's a journey, like life in general." The key for him, however, is to "trust your own inner voice." That keeps him from getting distracted by the noise of the world. "It's so personal," he says, which is why he feels it is so important to "stay true to your inner voice and give people what is coming from your heart." Applying that to the single "Icarus" he says, "I really honed in on what I wanted to say and what I wanted it to sound like. I knew that if I stayed true to what I was trying to say and do that somebody would relate to it."

Social media has definitely helped artists like Jason Pure reach the masses. He says, "It is a great tool that enables you to touch people that you can't necessary reach. I really have been trying to use it to connect with new audiences while continuing to maintain my current audience." Since the world is moving so fast, he adds: "You don't want to leave anyone behind."

Jason realizes that others can find a source of inspiration from what has worked for his own career.

"If you continue to put in the work, that work will show for itself eventually. Enjoy the process."

"Sometimes it can take the enjoyment out of it when you're almost too aware of your audience. That takes away from your creative authenticity." His goal moving forward? "Focus on what I'm trying to say, and make sure it is quality work." That noble sentiment is a great reminder for all of us that the old-fashioned virtue of "quality over quantity" should always be our goal.

1. Can your gift be a way for you to inspire and motivate others?

2. Like Jason, how can you have a positive outlook on your journey, even as you deal with the difficult moments?

Power Your Life WITH POSITIVITY

"People are just as happy as they make up their minds to be."

—Abraham Lincoln

Power Your Life BY ADDING VALUE

"If you wake up deciding what you want to give versus what you're going to get, you become a more successful person. In other words, if you want to make money, you have to help someone else make money.

—Russell Simmons

Power Your Life BY STAYING THE COURSE

"Hold on to your dreams of a better life and stay committed to striving to realize it."

—Earl G. Graves, Sr.

Power Your Life BY NOT GIVING UP

"I think a hero is an ordinary individual who finds the strength to persevere and endure in spite of overwhelming obstacles."

—Christopher Reeve

PROFILE #26:
HAVE A VISION AND WORK TOWARDS IT

Singer and TV Host Taylor Hicks

We have all experienced what are known as "full-circle moments": those things that start with us being in one place in our lives and, through challenges and accomplishments, lead us back stronger and more prepared for what's next. For Taylor Hicks, full-circle moments are what have made him the international sensation that people have gotten to know and love.

Since the Alabama native put the world under his spell, winning season five of *American Idol* in a finale that brought in over thirty million viewers, he has kept moving forward towards his purpose. As a platinum-selling recording artist, Taylor has been able to share his love of music with his fans and living the life that so many just dream about. In 2016, he added a new title to his name: television actor. Now in its second season, his TV show, *State Plate*, takes him across the country, bringing us some of America's most iconic food and interesting people.

There's just something about Taylor Hicks that draws you in. When I was offered the opportunity to interview Hicks, I knew that I wanted it to be about more than just his music. I wanted to present my readers with an opportunity to get to know the man behind the headlines, behind the success, and behind the music. I think we accomplished just that.

In this conversation we talked about the fans, the talent, and what he has to say about the process that has made his success possible—and which you can benefit from, too.

Hicks on the Impact of *American Idol*: "It changed my life. I mean, going from being a struggling artist and musician to being a household name." …

"It's one of those things I didn't take it for granted. I understood the business, and I know how hard it is to catch that big break."

"Obviously the break that I caught was one of the biggest in entertainment and television."

Hicks on Returning Home: "It's amazing. I mean, there's nothing like it. To have that kind of fan base and be on a show like *Idol* and come home is pretty awesome. I've been very blessed to have that opportunity."

Hicks on the Journey: "I think I was always singing as a kid, learning music. The love for music started at a very early age. I knew this was the path that I was going down. As a kid, I had a vision of being an artist—an entertainer—and being famous. When you have thought it all along and it happens, it's really easy to be yourself."

Hicks on Being Authentic: "I think that when you're talking about business, your relationships you have, and the people that are around you, they can tell if you are being real."

"As long as you are being true to yourself, you will be able to let people understand what that looks like and help them to see it's okay for them to be themselves."

"People who really know you for you, that is something that definitely helps you. It keeps you grounded. The people who knew you 'when' are the best."

Hicks on the Responsibility to His Fans and the Music: "I feel really blessed and thankful for those who voted for me and have supported me in my career as an artist. If it wasn't for the fans, in my business, I wouldn't be here. I have to respect what they have to say, listen to them, and let them be a part of what I have going on. It's important that I have undeniably great music. I think with me and the way that I feel about releasing a product or an album is not to dilute it.

I don't want to release stuff that may not be as great as it can be. That's what I'm going to do with this next album. I think this should be what every artist should strive, to put as much of their own influence on their art as possible."

Hicks' Advice for All Those With a Passion: "I've lived the American dream. You have to get a lot of 'Nos' before you get the one 'Yes.' It's something you have to take to heart and really have the vision to carry it through, whether it's singing, dancing, writing, business or whatever."

"Take it from me: I've had a lot of 'Nos', but all it takes is that one yes and you're on your way."

1. How can you look for opportunities to be a better version of yourself?

2. What changes are you willing to make in order to get to a more positive, productive place?

Power Your Life BY GETTING YOURSELF OUT THERE

"I had to make my own living and my own opportunity. But I made it! Don't sit down and wait for the opportunities to come. Get up and make them."

—Madam C.J. Walker

Power Your Life WITH TRANSFORMATION

"Our strength grows out of our weakness."

—Ralph Waldo Emerson

Power Your Life WITH TRIUMPH OVER STRUGGLE

"Only through experience of trial and suffering can the soul be strengthened, vision cleared, ambition inspired, and success achieved."

—Helen Keller

Power Your Life WITH THE POWER OF LOVE

"To love is to act."

—Victor Hugo

PROFILE #27:
SHINE YOUR LIGHT NO MATTER WHERE YOU ARE

Writer and Producer Will Packer

He has has brought the world some of the most entertaining box office successes, including *Stomp the Yard*, *Think Like A Man*, *Think Like A Man Too*, *Takers*, *No Good Deed*, and *The Wedding Ringer*, as well as 2017's *Girl's Trip*—and there's no sign that Will Packer is slowing down any time soon. In 2018, he will be bringing special programming to OWN: The Oprah Winfrey Network, expanding on his brand.

Will Packer has worked with some of the brightest stars in Hollywood, and in the process has made a name for himself as one of the "go-to" guys for quality projects that break stereotypes and records. "This is a challenging industry," he says. "It's tough to get into, and tough to maintain a level of success once you are in. It's a lot of hard work."

The hard work has been paying off big for Packer: critics and movie goers alike have responded favorably to his work on the screen. He says the response is a "true validation" for his dedication to the craft. "That's the kind of validation you hope for when you are working those long hours. You hope for that kind of validation, so it feels good when you get it."

When discussing how he has been able to make his mark in Hollywood without being changed by the industry, Packer says the key is that he makes time to "get out of the Hollywood bubble" and visit his home in Atlanta. By doing this, he is also showing that you can work in Hollywood and not have to become "Hollywood" in order to "make it."

Packer also makes the time to give back as much as possible, paying it forward for the next generation. "I take the opportunity to try to work with others who have shown that they have what it takes," he says.

"You can't help everybody, but you can lead by example. I try to set an example of what it takes to be successful in this industry."

For him the ingredients include "hard work, having good people around you and having a lot of faith."

His advice for anyone who wants to be successful in whatever they are doing? "You never know where you are going to end up. Whatever you are doing, give it 110 percent. You can't just decide one day to start being great. You have to give 110 percent every day, even if it's a job that you don't particularly love. When the opportunity arises, you got to be ready for it. You have to be used to always working hard."

1. Like Will, can you look for ways to create opportunities for your gift to be used?

2. What rewards have you experienced that maybe you have taken for granted that can be a reminder for you as to what is possible?

Power Your Life BY TAKING THE TOUGH ROAD

"The right path is very steep upward, whereas the wrong path is horizontal."

—Mizo proverb

Power Your Life WITH INTUITION

"Have the courage to follow your heart and intuition. They somehow already know what you truly want to become. Everything else is secondary."

—Steve Jobs

Power Your Life WITH HARD WORK

"People from all walks of life and all over the world look at me and know my humble beginnings and know that everything I've done has been through hard work. People respect me as a marketer and brand builder."

—Sean Combs

Power Your Life BY TAKING ACTION

"We're going to have to dig deep into our souls, confront our own self-doubt, and recognize that our destiny is in our hands —that our future is what we make of it."

—Michelle Obama

PROFILE #28:
BE UNAPOLOGETICALLY YOU

Singer and TV Personality Aubrey O'Day

In spite of the difficulties and challenges they face, some people just seemed destined for greatness. Aubrey O'Day is one of those people.

You have gotten to know her from the hit MTV show *Making the Band* and the chart-topping group Danity Kane. But she is also a star on Broadway and has her own reality show (*All About Aubrey*), and has been a contestant on the hit show *Celebrity Apprentice*. No matter what she does, it appears that Ms. O'Day is living her life out loud and enjoying the benefits of doing so.

"I never underestimate my fans," Aubrey said to me when discussing her number-one solo album and the other projects she has been a part of. "They're pretty amazing. I have a group called the Aubtourage who are always there at a moment's notice. They have become my lifeline." She added, "It's been great to see how much they reward everything that I'm a part of."

The honesty in which Aubrey lives is not new, and it is obviously part of the appeal she holds for her fans. They like her realness. "I have always had a pretty distinct, fearless voice," she told me.

> *"I'm someone you either love or love to hate. I've never been an in-between person."*

"Sometimes I get to a place where I have regrets and think if I wasn't so opinionated I'd have more support across the board, but that wouldn't be me."

> *"I am who I am. As I have gotten older, I've become more proud of that and less willing to make excuses for it."*

Listening to her explain the way she sees herself, I asked Aubrey about what she sees as her purpose in life. The answer was surprising for me. "I think that over being a singer, actress, or TV personality, the one thing that I have always wanted to be is a person that touches as many lives as I can before I die. The only way you can do that is by being honest."

Honesty is at the core of not just Aubrey's album but her daily walk as well.

> *"Whenever you are honest to who you are you always win in life,"* she says.

"Whether it's the way you thought or something more brilliant than what you expected. Having your own authentic voice is key."

1. How can being honest in your pursuit of a more positive life help you get to where you want to go?

2. Aubrey has been able to inspire others by just being the best version of herself, and staying positive about making that brave choice. How can you mirror that in your own life?

Power Your Life WITH PASSION

"When I was younger there was something in me. I had passion. I may not have known what I was going to do with that passion, but there was something—and I still feel it. It's this little engine that roars inside of me and I just want to keep going and going."

—Sheila Johnson

Power Your Life BY STANDING UP FOR YOU

"Learn to value yourself, which means: fight for your happiness."

—Ayn Rand

Power Your Life BY TRUSTING THE PROCESS

"You cannot force ideas. Successful ideas are the result of slow growth. Ideas do not reach perfection in a day, no matter how much study is put upon them."

—Alexander Graham Bell

Power Your Life WITH FRIENDSHIPS

"The better part of one's life consists of his friendships."

—Abraham Lincoln

PROFILE #29:
YOU'RE NEVER TOO YOUNG (OR OLD) TO START AGAIN

Author Mary Higgins Clark

When it comes to pursuing your goals and dreams without excuses—and powering your life with the positive—international bestselling author Mary Higgins Clark is a shining example of achievement and inspiration. At the age of ninety, she is still writing books, setting records, and entertaining readers around the world.

I had the opportunity to speak with her twice during 2017. The last time was right after the release of her newest book, *Every Breath You Take*. We talked not just about her fans, but also about the authors she has inspired along the way.

When it comes to her amazing writing career, she told me: "People say to me all the time, 'You're ninety. Why don't you give it up?' I tell them I love writing and I get paid well for it, so why should I stop?"

> *Writing was something that Ms. Clark has always known was a part of who she is.*

"I was writing skits for my brother to perform when I was quite young," she says. "Even in school I wasn't the best at certain subjects, but writing I excelled at."

Ms. Clark loves hearing from her fans and meeting them at events, but there is one thing she has no time for: excuses. She told me she has people tell her they want to do this or that but don't have time or feel as though they might be too old. "There is no excuse for not following your dream," she says. "I had five children when my husband died of a heart attack. I still got up early and wrote for over an hour before having to go to work."

She continued: "Time is something you can make work. If you're a night person, then write at night after everyone has gone to bed. If you're an early riser, make time for what you love in the morning. And if you are a person of a certain age, think about what your sharing your gift with your family could mean for them. There is nothing like being able to bring joy to others, so don't let excuses be the reason why you don't do it."

1. What excuse can you remove in pursuing the things you want in your life?

2. How can you, like Ms. Clark, change your perspective on a seemingly frustrating situation you face and turn it into a positive?

Power Your Life WITH A GOOD ATTITUDE

> **"It is very important to generate a good attitude, a good heart, as much as possible. From this, happiness in both the short term and the long term for both yourself and others will come."**
>
> **—14th Dalai Lama**

Power Your Life BY SEIZING THE DAY

> **"The life so short, the craft so long to learn."**
>
> **—Hippocrates**

Power Your Life BY NOT WASTING TIME

> **"If you love life, don't waste time, for time is what life is made up of."**
>
> **—Bruce Lee**

Power Your Life WITH A SENSE OF WONDER

"Though we travel the world over to find the beautiful, we must carry it with us, or we find it not."

—Ralph Waldo Emerson

PROFILE #30:
GET OUT OF YOUR OWN WAY

Author Wally Lamb

Success can be an interesting thing. As you have seen in other examples in this book, life is full of uncertainty. What matters is how you show up for every situation. A great example of this comes from bestselling author Wally Lamb. His books *She's Come Undone* and *I Know This Much Is True* were runaway successes (and Oprah's Book Club selections!), but what would happen with his future releases? Would he have the same response? Can we expect everything to go as it has in the past? That is part of what Wally and I discussed during our conversation together.

CW. What has it been like for you to be able to reflect not only on your own journey but also how people around you have contributed to who you are?

WL. Well, you know, if you put a writer by himself in front of a computer you would be surprised at how much comes up from the imagination and yourself. I am at this stage of my life where I enjoy looking back, and kind of trying to figure it (life) all out.

CW. Do you think one of the reasons why you have had the success that you have had is because you make your characters so "us?!" You make them so that they are not perfect: they have their issues, but they are also on a journey like all of us can relate to?

WL. Yes, you know, I think the thing that connects me to all the characters I have created over the years is ...

We are imperfect people who are laboring and trying to figure out how to become better people. I feel that we are all sort of works in progress.

If you are not stretching and growing beyond the limitations of who you were maybe ten or twenty years ago then you are stagnant. So that's what I like—is to create a character I am never sure where that character is going in the novel. I am always a little bit envious of novelists who has the whole thing plotted out and outlined and they know exactly that they are writing towards a specified end, but it doesn't work that way for me, so I'm kind of like sitting in the passenger seat along with the protagonist who is driving the car and taking me on a ride ... and I am not sure where that ride is going to go.

CW. What has that part of your experience been like for you as you've been able to find your place in the world and see how others respond?

WL. I love that. I think it's really cool. I guess probably in terms of media what sort of rocketed me onto the national stage was the fact that one day, out of the blue, Oprah Winfrey called up and said she had picked my first novel, *She's Come Undone*, for her book club. Now my books are selling in the millions because of her endorsements. You know, the irony didn't escape me that when television came around it was supposed to be the end of reading. There was a lot of doom and gloom about that, but really it was a television show that brought me so many more readers.

CW. Really good point. I want to ask you this with that I mind, Wally. In the face of all the success that you have had, how has Wally Lamb been able to focus on what really matters?

WL.

> *Well, you know, I think that I was blessed in that my success as a novelist came later in my life.*

I was a high school English teacher for about twenty-five years, and I started writing on the side actually. I started the very same day our first kid was born, so I've been at it for a while, but I think had I been an overnight success when I was in my twenties as a young novelist I could have really been a jerk about things. But there is something that living for a little while longer and sort of being grounded—very much grounded—by a family that keeps me humble. I've always been grateful for that. My success came when I was in my forties as opposed to earlier, and so at that point you know I had aging parent; I had a wonderful book contract to write more books, but also [wanted] to give something back to the universe because it had been so good to me.

I appreciate everything, and that is how I look at each day. With appreciation.

1. How can you look at this day as a new beginning?

2. What really matters the most in your life, and how can you spend more time with that?

Power Your Life BY ACCEPTING YOUR IMPERFECTIONS

"The blessed work of helping the world forward, happily does not wait to be done by perfect men."

—George Eliot

Power Your Life WITH HOPE

"Optimism is the faith that leads to achievement; nothing can be done without hope."

—Helen Keller

Power Your Life WITH GRATITUDE FOR LIFE

"Every day above earth is a good day."

—Ernest Hemingway

Power Your Life WITH TOGETHERNESS

"Alone we can do so little. Together we can do so much. Only love can break down the walls that stand between us and our happiness."

—Helen Keller

PROFILE #31:
RECOGNIZE WHAT MAKES YOU UNIQUE

Actor Jon Chaffin

For actor Jon Chaffin, acting has been the vehicle to not just living his dreams but inspiring others to do the same. He been able to play a variety of roles, from the tough guy, to the funny guy, to the good guy. It is in the role of Warlock "War" Lewis on Tyler Perry's *The Haves and the Have Nots*, however, that the world has taken notice of Jon. After just one episode, he became a fan favorite. He left the show in 2017, but had definitely made his mark.

"We, as actors, live for the chance to slip into different roles and do things in this imaginary world that we don't do in real life," he told me during our conversation together. "It's always an honor when I am able to play certain roles."

Jon described acting to me as being able to "get back to that childlike stage when I just do things so it comes naturally." That has really been the key for him along his path.

Looking at the success of the show *The Haves and the Have Nots*, Jon says "It's been an awesome experience. Nothing short of spectacular." Working with the cast has really made the project worthwhile for him.

"When you have good people to get along with it makes for an easy work environment where everyone can put forth their best work."

After visiting with him in Los Angeles, here are some other nuggets from our conversation that I think should spark some positive thoughts for your own journey:

Jon's Inspiration for Acting: "Movies like *The Five Heartbeats* and *The Shawshank Redemption* made me want to act. Individuals like Robert Townsend inspired me. What they did with that movie (*Five Heartbeats*) drew me in. I would actually quote the movie. I had watched it so much I could quote each character. There were times I would perform certain scenes for my family. Having that imaginative world to get lost in was my first real "aha moment" when I said I want to do this."

Jon on Portraying Warlock on Tyler Perry's *The Haves and the Have Nots*: "We are representing real life. There are real Warlocks in the world. Portraying him allow me to put on different shoes and wear different hats and challenge myself.

"I don't play stereotypes. I play people. This person (Warlock) was someone who had her (Candace Young, played by Tika Sumpter) back. Everyone wants that—to have somebody that you can go to is important. I had no idea that they (viewers of the show) would fall in love with Warlock after one episode!"

Jon's Idea of Success:

"For me, it's just about doing what my heart's desire is. If I can wake up and do this and pursue this I'm successful."

"Everybody wants different things. As I continue to grow in my career, I noticed that my success is predicated on my happiness. Success is not necessarily how many people know your name. It's more or less are you able to do something that you love."

Jon's Advice for You: "Identify what your desire is and accept that you can have that."

"I believe that whatever is in my heart that brings me joy is what God has for me."

"When I'm on set and I'm happy that lets me know I'm in alignment."

"Find what makes you happy. Be bold. Be daring. Do it. You have to take a chance on yourself."

1. How can you look at the layers of your own life and spend more time on the areas that you want to enhance?

2. Jon encouraged you to find what makes you happy. What are some of those things and how can that help change your life in a more positive way?

Power Your Life WITH A SENSE OF WONDER

"Find things beautiful as much as you can, most people find too little beautiful."

—Vincent Van Gogh

Power Your Life BY BEING IN THE MOMENT

"Seize the moments of happiness, love and be loved! That is the only reality in the world, all else is folly."

—Leo Tolstoy

Power Your Life BY SHARING THE LOVE

"Those who bring sunshine into the lives of others cannot keep it from themselves."

—J.M. Barrie

Power Your Life WITH SELF-RESPONSIBILITY

"What I learned at a very early age was that I was responsible for my life."

—Oprah Winfrey

PROFILE #32:
BE AN EXAMPLE BY CELEBRATING OTHERS

Singer and Actress Stephanie Mills

I have interviewed almost eight thousand guests over the past fifteen years, and Grammy Award-winning singer and actress Stephanie Mills is by far one of the most dynamic and positive forces I have encountered. She has accomplished so much, but none of it has gone to her head.

She has granted me two conversations, the last time being in 2017, just days before Atlanta recognized September 29, 2017 as "Stephanie Mills Day." Each time we met, she was aware of her accomplishments but looking forward to what was to come. That is what this conversation was all about.

CW. Ms. Mills, I tell people after our first conversation how surprised I was of your humility when it came to your accomplishments. It's really an example for all of us as to how we should see ourselves. As you look at your forty years in the business, do you still have those wow moments as to how your life has unfolded?

SM. Thank you for saying that, but I don't really look back. I appreciate and enjoy so much what I do. I enjoy live performing. I enjoy doing theater and I just, I am thankful that I am able to still do it and enjoy it.

> *I still get nervous when I go on stage, and I like that feeling because that means I am not tainted by my success.*

I don't take it for granted.

CW. I think that in itself says so much as well. You mentioned being out on stage, and you have the benefit of having such a diverse audience. What is that like for you, to look out in the audience and to see these people of all ages that all love your music and can sing your music along with you?

SM. It's mind-blowing, because when kids come up to me and say, "I know who you are!" or, "I like your music," I am like, "You are too young to know who I am!" but their mothers teach them and play my music. That makes me feel really, really good that I am reaching this generation.

CW. Right, and another way that you have been able to do that is because of social media, and I think having a presence there has definitely helped people to kind of be able to stay connected with everything going on with you. What has that been like for you, to navigate and to kind of think about how now in real time we are able to stay connected the way that we are?

SM. I love it. I love Twitter. I love Instagram. I like being able to wake up sometimes and just say good morning, because I call my fans love bugs—and I like being able to say "Good morning, love bugs." I use mine purely for professional reasons. I don't like the personal side so much, but I love to be able to tell them when shows are and if I have something coming out, or if I've heard music that I think they would enjoy.

CW. And the support that you give to others I think is another thing that again we can all learn from. I mean that Sisterhood and the bond especially supporting other women in the business. Has that always been something that you knew you wanted to do?

SM. Absolutely.

I would love to do a tour with me and some of my sister friends. I think it's very, very important that we support each other.

I don't think that we should be jealous of each other or throw shade at each other, because we are all uniquely different, and there is enough out here for everybody, so I really always try to support.

CW. What do you think has helped you to be that way, Ms. Mills?

SM. My faith, and just staying true to who I am, not living too big.

> *I love what I do, but I don't do it for the fame. I've never done it for the fame.*

I really love to just sing and perform and be out there with my band and other entertainers. I just love doing simple things, and I think if you keep it simple and you don't get caught up in the hype, don't get caught up in thinking that you are better. We are blessed and privileged. We live a very privileged life, so to me I think we should always stay humble.

I've had my trials and my tribulations. I am not trying to make it sound like everything in my life has been easy, but I've always tried to adjust.

> *The one thing, the one consistent thing in my life that has kept it good for me, is my faith in God. Without Him I am nothing.*

1. What about Ms. Mills' journey most impressed you?

2. How can you think less about the trials in your life and more about what is possible?

Power Your Life WITH HOPE

**"Hope" is the thing with feathers—
That perches in the soul—And sings
the tune without the words—
And never stops—at all[.]**

—Emily Dickinson

Power Your Life BY TRUSTING IN YOUR STRENGTH

"When I dare to be powerful—to use my strength in the service of my vision, then it becomes less and less important whether I am afraid."

—Audre Lorde

Power Your Life WITH FEARLESS SELF-GROWTH

"The battles that count aren't the ones for gold medals. The struggles within yourself--the invisible, inevitable battles inside all of us— that's where it's at."

—Jesse Owens

Power Your Life WITH SELF-KNOWLEDGE

"It is not possible to scan the universe as it is to scan the self. Know the self and you know the universe."

—Ghandi

PROFILE #33:
THE ROAD TO SUCCESS IS LONG BUT WORTH IT

Actress Renee Lawless

She may have become known to many through her work on stage, but 2013 has solidified the status of actress Renee Lawless as one of the unforgettable stars on Tyler Perry's runaway hit *The Haves and the Have Nots*.

In the first ten minutes of the show's first episode, we saw her character Katheryn Cryer being the strong matriarch of her family; however, the show has also revealed another side of the woman whose cutting retorts and strength mask a world of hurt and pain. Millions have made the show must-see television, and Renee couldn't be happier. She and I connected soon after *The Haves and the Have Nots* started, and for the past five years we have stayed in touch—and I am glad to call her a friend. In fact, after my grandmother died in 2014, she was one of the cast members from show who reached out to me, offering her condolences.

In one of our most recent chats in 2017, I asked about her thoughts on the first episode and the audience reaction to it. Her answer?

"This is going to be a hit, and I'm a part of it."

Renee went on to tell me that they expected high numbers on the first season, and that as their audience has continued to grow it has really been more overwhelming. The drama is groundbreaking: it's the Oprah Winfrey Network's first scripted drama, and the first of three projects created by Tyler Perry that appear on OWN. The importance of this moment is not lost on Renee.

"Not too many people get to be at the start of something great," she said to me.

Renee Lawless' place in the spotlight is something that has been in the works for quite some time.

"Even as a young child I was singing the loudest in church plays," she told me.

"I always dreamed of being a movie star." When she began in theater, it just felt right to her. "This is my home," she said of the experience. "This is where I want to be." She knew in high school that no matter where she went, performing would be a part of her life. "I've been on stage many years, but my ultimate goal was always TV and eventually film." *The Haves and the Have Nots* has made that dream come true. She said that to not only have achieved her ultimate goal of being a series regular, but to be a star of a series, is an experience she is loving.

It was really intriguing to talk with Renee about how she has brought Katheryn to life. "I knew all these layers before you all did," she told me. "With any new television drama, everyone is brought in in the middle. It's up to the characters to bring you in. The one thing that I love about Katheryn is that she's a very multi-layered person—it's like peeling back layers of an onion. She's like a hollow oak tree: outside, she's a strong pillar of strength—but on the inside she's rotting and hollow. What her husband and children and life have given her has made her a very lonely person. It's basically what it means to have and to have not."

Renee then gave an example that I think resonates with everyone. "Even though she's worth fifty million dollars, she's a woman who's over a certain age, who doesn't like getting old, who is dealing with cancer and problems with her kids. Not many can relate to being worth fifty million dollars, but fifty million people can relate to what she's going through. She in many ways is one of the most relatable characters because she has all of these layers. She's just like me."

Though things are going well for Renee and she is doing what she loves, it hasn't happened without a real commitment to her craft. "I worked very hard and long and got many more rejections than I've had successes," she told me.

> *"I do this because I love it, not for the award or the pay check that it affords me."*

Speaking of the world that actors live in, she adds: "Our career is very unsure. If you're just doing it for the fame and glory you're not going to go very far or last." Her next words are great reminders for all of us with a dream.

> *"You have to love what you do in order to truly be successful at it."*

May those words resonate with us as we identify our passion in life and vow to pursue it.

1. What is one thing you have done that just felt right, like something you were meant to do?

2. Renee talks about being practical. How can you do the same, in a way that honors who you are and what you want in life?

Power Your Life BY SPEAKING YOUR TRUTH

"The truth is the kindest thing we can give folks in the end."

—Harriet Beecher Stowe

Power Your Life WITH GRIT

"Just don't give up what you're trying to do. Where there is love and inspiration, I don't think you can go wrong."

—Ella Fitzgerald

Power Your Life BY TRUSTING YOUR FEELINGS

"Human feeling is like the mighty rivers that bless the earth: it does not wait for beauty — it flows with resistless force and brings beauty with it."

—George Eliot

Power Your Life WITH CURIOSITY

"Life was meant to be lived, and curiosity must be kept alive. One must never, for whatever reason, turn his back on life."

—Eleanor Roosevelt

PROFILE #34:
BELIEVE YOU CAN DO IT

Model and Actor Anthony C. Johns

Model and actor Anthony C. Johns is all about challenging himself to set goals, moving past obstacles, and showing others what is possible. He has travelled the world, worked with some of the best photographers in the industry, walked runways, and amassed fans from around the world—and he is only just getting started.

When I caught up with him at the end of 2017, he was in the States taking a break from his whirlwind career and was able to reflect a bit on the life he has been able to live. "I would say that my progress has been based on a spiritual foundation," he told me. One of the things that has helped him was the book *The Purpose-Driven Life*. "It really changed my aspect on what I can do, when I can do it and believing in myself."

The road has not always been easy, but Anthony is no stranger to overcoming difficult situations.

"I've been able to accomplish my goals through hard work and patience and going through rejection," he says. "It has made me a better person."

Anthony became interested in modeling and acting when he was just a kid. He says he has always seen the two as "a reflection of life." The emotional reaction involved appealed to him, and he became motivated by seeing what you can create. With the reward, however, has come the obvious challenge of just being thought of by how you look. "That's when it becomes pretty difficult for me," he admits, "when the titles come, and you have to live up to it."

Though he says the compliments about his body can fuel the ego, he says he works hard to stay humble at the same time realizing how soon it can all be gone.

As with any art, Anthony has come to see his body as his canvas. That means he has to take care of it in order to be the best he can be in his industry. That also means being comfortable in his own skin and realizing what he has to offer. "That was a major obstacle when I first wanted to do the business of modeling," he told me. "I was at a point in my life when I was comparing myself to other models."

I learned to create my own self-representation by working on my mind, body and soul."

Today he says he believes in confidence that begins from within—and that kind of confidence is what comes across in the work he does. "My progress came through seeing myself improving in the way I lived, eat, and balance life."

"I saw myself grow by getting out of the box, doing jobs that are challenging, pretty much confronting what was an obstacle for me."

What Anthony has achieved has been noted beyond the circle of those who admire his work. He has become an inspiration for others. "I am a role model," he declared. "I am a person who has power," and he realizes that power is not just for him. "I wanted to use my gifts to help others. Those people have become my recipe to keep it going."

"I am making a difference. It's really not about me. It's a calling I must fulfill."

"If I'm doing this and I'm not helping other people, then I am doing something wrong."

1. How can you use your personal power to better affect the world around you?

2. If you were to focus on ways you can help others and not just yourself, would that help you live a more positive life?

Power Your Life WITH ACTS OF KINDNESS

"No act of kindness, no matter how small, is ever wasted."

—Aesop

Power Your Life BY PUTTING IN THE WORK

"Just remember, you can do anything you set your mind to, but it takes action, perseverance, and facing your fears."

—Gillian Anderson

Power Your Life WITH PATIENCE

"He that can have patience can have what he will."

—Benjamin Franklin

Power Your Life WITH JOY

"Joy is compassion. Joy is giving yourself to somebody else, or something else. And it's a kind of thing that is, in its subtlety and lowness, much more powerful than pleasure. [...] If you pursue joy; you will find everlasting happiness."

—George Lucas

PROFILE #35:
YOUR LIFE CAN CHANGE THE WORLD

Singer Kenny Lattimore

The New York Times may have said it best when it called Kenny Lattimore the "Modern Soul Man."

In 2017, he released a highly anticipated album entitled *Vulnerable*, and it was exactly what his fans have come to expect. At the time this book was being published, Lattimore was celebrating his new single "Stay on Your Mind." This musician, who is known for sultry love songs that will stimulate your mind and give the guys something to recite to that special lady, is back with new music—and he is sharing all that he is with all of us.

The past few years, he has literally been around the world and back again, meeting his fans, sharing his music and his talents on stage, and showing us all what it means to live life on purpose. Getting this interview with Lattimore at the start of 2018 was not only an honor for me, but something that I knew lovers of music would enjoy ... along with anyone looking for an example of what is possible in relationships and in life. In this man, we see an example of both.

In one of the most insightful conversations I've had, Kenny Lattimore takes us into the depths of who he is and strives to be, and what he hopes for all of us as well.

Lattimore on His Purpose: "I really feel that my musical purpose has been to speak to the hearts of women and the minds of men."

"It's been about my own personal journey, the way we approach communication and approach life."

"As I learn things and experience things I am able to put it in my music. I'm careful to give something for the ladies and not leave out my male listeners. I want the men to know that there is strength in wanting to know and understand women."

Lattimore on Being True to Yourself:

"One of the most difficult things was knowing my purpose when it wasn't popular."

"Knowing my musical purpose was more than what was sometimes expected—I had to keep rolling and stay true to myself, not allowing anyone to deter me. As I have matured, I have been able to embrace it more. There's no getting around this simple fact: God calls you to a purpose.

"Music is a platform of communication. I had strong ideals about love and what love should be, but I wasn't always sure how I wanted to translate that fully. I had to get comfortable. As you live you get better."

"As an artist, there is a certain sense of vulnerability that we have to accept."

"Everything you want to do is not always going to translate. Your purpose can't be to fulfill myself. It has to be to give to others. That's what I have been working on over the years."

Lattimore on His Greatest Passion: "I would have to say that my greatest passion is mentoring and giving information. As a mentor, you become very protective of people. Through the platform I have, I am able to talk freely about the things I am passionate about."

Lattimore on New Music: "I appreciate you (the fans), even when I have been trying to figure it out. The fans believed that whatever I did, I would continue to come with a certain quality. For me, it is about being able to build a legacy that is reputable and respected."

Lattimore on Staying True to the Purpose: "It's tough when the world is going in a particular direction and you may feel as though you are out there by yourself."

"The important thing is making decisions that let you know you are doing the right thing. It might not be easy."

"It takes the consistently to understand who you are and be strong in that. Embrace where you are supposed to go. There is a tremendous blessing in embracing your purpose."

Lattimore on Your Dream: "Despise not the day of small beginnings. That is what I say to people who are trying to figure it out. God delights when we start. We sometimes think everything has to be lined up a certain way. Even when you don't understand your purpose you can discover it and walk in it."

1. How can you identify your purpose and make a plan to stay true to it?

2. Kenny talks about the importance of starting on your course. What will you do today to make steps towards a more positive outlook?

Power Your Life BY BELIEVING IN YOURSELF

"Whatever we believe about ourselves
and our ability comes true for us."

—Susan L. Taylor, journalist

Power Your Life BY SEEING PEOPLE AS PEOPLE

"In recognizing the humanity of our
fellow beings, we pay ourselves the
highest tribute."

—Thurgood Marshall

Power Your Life BY CHOOSING LOVE OVER HATE

"Hatred paralyzes life; love releases it.
Hatred confuses life; love harmonizes it.
Hatred darkens life; love illuminates it."

—Martin Luther King, Jr.

Power Your Life BY STAYING TRUE TO YOUR ROOTS

"Change your opinions, keep to your principles; change your leaves, keep intact your roots."

—Victor Hugo

PROFILE #36:
USE YOUR SPOTLIGHT TO LIGHT THE WAY FOR OTHERS

Media Personality and Author Leeza Gibbons

Over the years, one of the greatest blessings I have received in my life is appreciating the gift of today. It allows me to remember that although yesterday wasn't perfect, my life is not over as long as I have breath in my body. Though today presents us with a great opportunity, it also gives us the choice to foolishly waste it, repeating the mistakes and choices that we have already made. Sometimes it's easy to give up and hard to choose the right, especially when it feels like you are the only person struggling.

One of the individuals I myself look to as a source of inspiration is Leeza Gibbons. I've gone from just being a fan of her work to being able to call her a friend. She has supported my work over the years, and the way she radiates positivity is contagious. In 2016, she released her book *Fierce Optimism*. It was my pleasure to have a conversation with her, not just about the

book but her own lessons learned along her
incredible journey.

What has been the secret to Leeza's success? "I think in
life we get exactly what we are willing to put up with,"
she told me.

*"If you don't respect yourself, then you can't expect
anyone else to honor who you want to be in the
world. We teach people how to treat us. You have to
value who you are."*

This takes work. It takes effort. This reminds us that
anything worth having is going to require some work
on our part. "Whether you are trying to recreate your
life or invent a new product, you have to drop the
dread and you have to banish the blame," says Leeza.
In her book, she refers to this decision as a form of
rebooting. "That's the biggest option we have," she told
me. "It comes down to thinking." She gave examples
of individuals who were all great at their professions.
"The one thing they all have in common is they know
how to think."

*"When you change the way you think, everything
else in your life will adapt."*

What Leeza shared reminded me of what she wrote in her 2013 book, *Take 2 : Your Guide to Creating Happy Endings and New Beginnings*, in a chapter entitled "Ask Yourself: Are You Worth It?" A section called "Who Do You Think You Are?" began it with this profound statement:

> *"How we see ourselves is exactly who we'll become."*

This has a great deal to do with the story we tell ourselves about ourselves.

"You do have to have a real sense of who you are and a real foundation," Leeza said to me. "You have to run your own race and don't worry about what others are doing." She then shared something that I hadn't thought about before—having a mission statement for your life.

> *"Take some time to really write down what you want and who you are,"* she urged.

"We do it in business, and we should do the same for ourselves." Our mission statement should include how you interact with the world and how you want the world to see you. If you do this, Leeza says you will then know better who you are and where your lines in the sand are.

It's obvious that someone like Leeza is setting an example for men and women alike, when it comes to the course she is on. I asked her what it was like to know that she was an inspiration to others. "I think that when we are of service then we really do feel productive and proud," she answered. "I finally got to the place where I said how I am received is not my work. My work is to embrace it and put it out there."

Writing for Leeza isn't about saying everything for her was perfect. It is more about showing a path and focusing on moving towards a better way of looking at life. "Where we put our intention and attention is where things go," Leeza says.

"Where focus goes, energy flows."

This is important to keep in mind even when we make mistakes. "If you never fail, then you're not taking enough risks in your life. All successes are built on failures." Leeza says we cheat ourselves when we hold off starting something, simply because of the fear of failure. In her opinion, it is better to try and fail— and then build on that failure moving forward.

"Anytime I need to feel connection and to recognize that there a greater power at play in my life, I pray," she says. "Often I ask for strength and wisdom and to have an open mind to recognize God's messages to me. I think so often we pray for something, but we don't like the response, so we deny it. I pray that I will accept the reply and recognize that no is an answer, too."

"Perspective is a beautiful thing."

Leeza said as we wrapped up our time together: "It's about learning to be in gracious acceptance. Real strength comes from knowing your limits. Be quiet and allow answers to come in." This definitely requires a bit of faith on our part. "We can only know so much," she says.

"People who are happy don't see the top of the staircase, but they keep climbing anyway."

Her advice to you: "This is your moment. Don't wait for some far-off time when the alarm will ring and you'll suddenly know to step out of the shadows and into the spotlight." All of us can begin walking towards that spotlight right now. It all begins with the choice to do so.

1. Who is someone you can look to as an example of what a more positive, balanced life looks like?

2. How can you begin to step out of the shadows today?

Power Your Life WITH THE POWER OF YOUR DREAMS

"Never underestimate the power of dreams and the influence of the human spirit. We are all the same in this notion: The potential for greatness lives within each of us."

—Wilma Rudolph

Power Your Life BY MAKING CHANGE HAPPEN

"Change will not come if we wait for some other person or some other time. We are the ones we've been waiting for. We are the change that we seek."

—Barack Obama

Power Your Life BY BEING POSITIVE

"Live, and be happy, and make others so."

—Mary Shelley

Power Your Life BY BEING CONSTRUCTIVE

"It has always been easy to hate and destroy. To build and to cherish is much more difficult."

—Queen Elizabeth

PROFILE #37:
BE BOLD. BE BRAVE. BE YOU.

Poet and Author Joy Elan

"Anything is possible."

Yes, I know we hear that all the time, but I have found it to be so true, especially if you have the right tools and know how to use them. Take, for example, Joy Elan. She is legally deaf, but that has not stopped her from being an award-winning poet, spoken word artist and author—and she's not done yet.

When I caught up with Joy in 2017, we talked about all that she had been able to achieve, including releasing her first novel. "It's amazing," she says, "and some of it I couldn't believe that I accomplished."

Part of what made 2016 such a great year for her was that she was able to introduce her poetry to a younger audience by making some slight adjustments. "I knew I needed to clean up the language and the content to reach another audience," she said. "That helped me propel and take off even more." Realizing that she could still deliver powerful messages without using what some might call "strong language," Joy said that she realized she was limiting her audience before.

> *It all began by speaking honestly to herself.*

"I'm supposed to be an educator. Why do I have all this foul language in my writing? Time for me to grow up a little. I wanted something that everyone could read." What was the big lesson that this changed revealed? "It made me realize that

in order to be marketable you have to be accessible."

During the conversation, I shifted the attention to how Joy has been able to do what she has without allowing the fear of failure to stop her. "I'm my own determining factor," she told me.

> *"Life is a very interesting thing. You either believe you can do it or you can't."*

"I don't wait for other people to tell me. I go based on when I'm ready. It's all based on my inspiration and motivation. I've always been like this as a person," she said. "Once I put my mind to something I do it. I have to believe in myself. I can't wait on anybody else."

Another motivation for Joy is her daughter. "She's part of the reason why I do what I do," she said during her interview. "I don't want to just tell her to go after her dreams. I want her to see me doing it. She sees me working around the clock. This is hard work and takes dedication. Things come when you put time and energy to it."

That is the message she wants everyone to get. "I want to be an example of someone who can have a goal or dream and see it come true. When I leave this earth my words will live on forever. I don't care where you're from or what kind of situation you are in, you have the power to make things happen for yourself. It might be hard, but if you really believe in something you will pursue it."

1. How can you eliminate the excuse of what you can't do and replace it with a courageous search for what is possible, even if it seems uncertain or overwhelming?

2. Part of Joy's motivation is her daughter. What in your life can you use to help motivate you?

Power Your Life WITH LOVE

"Love makes your soul crawl out from its hiding place."

—Zora Neale Hurston

Power Your Life BY FOLLOWING THROUGH

"Many people don't focus enough on execution. If you make a commitment to get something done, you need to follow through on that commitment."

—Kenneth Chenault

Power Your Life BY KNOWING THINGS CHANGE

"Pure and complete sorrow is as impossible as pure and complete joy."

—Leo Tolstoy

Power Your Life WITH SYMPATHY

"Everything bad that's ever happened to me has taught me compassion."

—Ellen DeGeneres

PROFILE #38:
MAKE SURE YOUR LIFE HAS THE RIGHT DIRECTOR

Director, Speaker and Author DeVon Franklin

It's been almost six years now since I turned on the television one particular Sunday morning for *Super Soul Sunday* on the Oprah Winfrey Network and became engrossed in Oprah's conversation with DeVon Franklin. The two were discussing his book *Produced by Faith*, and before the segment was over, I was on Amazon.com ordering the book and digesting the tips.

The premise of the conversation on OWN, as well as in the book, was all about direction and who we chose to take our lead from. Hearing Oprah talking to DeVon, it hit me just how timely a discussion this is for us to have today, when there are so many helpful and unhelpful things that try to control your life and monopolize your time. In the book *Produced by Faith*, Franklin discusses the importance of looking at your life as a movie, with our Heavenly Father being the greatest Director of all. Will we choose to listen to Him, or will we allow our egos to keep us from heeding the direction He gives? In 2017, he released a follow-up book, called *The Hollywood Commandments*.

I connected with DeVon, and the discussion that followed was not just inspiring, but was something I knew others needed to benefit from as well. There are some voices that need to be heard, and I knew one was speaking through DeVon Franklin.

When I asked him about the response to the books and the way his words were connecting with hearts and minds around the world, DeVon told me this: "It's been powerful. Being vocal about who I am and owning who God created me to be has contributed to my success in entertainment and guided me as I chart my own course in this business. I've learned and been able to share that when you put God first, everything else will fall into place."

In *Produced by Faith*, we are able to see how DeVon got to this place of not just being fearless in his faith but also how it has been rewarded. "Part of it came out of necessity," he told me when referring to the courage he was able to display.

"When something doesn't feel right it's very hard for me to do it."

When it came to assignments that made him unhappy and unfulfilled he says he recognized where the feeling was coming from. "I wasn't being my true self and operating in the confidence that God had given me," he said.

What helped DeVon to get on track? He did a self-examination.

"Out of necessity, I had to figure out how can I begin to start to like who I really am," he says. "Every time I tried to do my job as someone else it didn't work."

"I realized I had to do it the way I was built to do it. There is a danger when we feel like we have to emulate how someone else operates. You can't be successful if you are just emulating someone else. You have to find your own way of doing something."

How do we know that DeVon's perspective on his life and his dedication to his faith have worked? Consider the facts. At the time of our last conversation together he was celebrating not just the new book but also his movie, *The Star*. Before that he was serving as Senior Vice President of Production for Columbia Tristar Pictures, a division of Sony Pictures Entertainment, making him one of the youngest individuals in that position in the industry. He oversaw the remake of *Sparkle*, starring the late Whitney Houston in her last on-screen role, as well as *The Karate Kid*, which starred Jackie Chan and Jaden Smith. To quote a bit of Scripture, "By their fruits shall ye know them."

Since the release of his book, Franklin has been more out front in public, sharing what has worked for him. "Knowing that I'm created for a purpose, in these moments when I'm coming from behind the scenes I bring with me the knowledge I have taken in," he says. When looking at the success of his entertainment career and even the attention the books have gotten, he keeps things in their proper perspective.

"All these things that are happening to me are not about me," DeVon says. "It's really about God's time and God's will and knowing there are people that need to be reached."

By keeping his eye on the bigger picture, he has managed to keep his focus. "When you get lost, you lose sight of what originally motivated you in the first place," he explained. "It's always keeping purpose number one. It's about reaching people and being a servant. Long as I can keep that front and center, it continually helps me in making decisions. All of us have to make decisions that are rooted in purpose and what God wants you to do."

One of DeVon's favorite quotes is this:

"To get where you want to go, you've first got to become the person God wants you to be."

This takes effort but it is definitely worth the work involved. He says that his hope and prayer is that as you're looking at your life as a movie, with God as the director, it will give you the perspective to be an instrument of His plan. This means that we won't think the bad times we are going through are all there is to life. "The danger is that we think the scene we are in is permanent, when in fact it is temporary," he says. "In that permanent perception, we make decisions that can alter the direction of our story."

"All of us have practical things we can do to move from one scene in our lives to the next. We just have to trust that God knows our story from beginning to end."

1. Looking at your life as a movie, how can you change the next scene for the better?

2. Who is honestly directing your life currently, and how can you make sure that your "Director" help you be more positive about your life and the future, even if things are difficult now?

Power Your Life WITH BIG DREAMS

"I built a conglomerate and emerged the richest black man in the world in 2008 but it didn't happen overnight. It took me thirty years to get to where I am today. Youths of today aspire to be like me but they want to achieve it overnight. It's not going to work. To build a successful business, you must start small and dream big. In the journey of entrepreneurship, tenacity of purpose is supreme."

—Aliko Dangote

Power Your Life WITH COURAGE

"And each man stands with
his face in the light
Of his own drawn sword,
Ready to do what a hero can."

—Elizabeth Barrett Browning

Power Your Life WITH YOUR INDIVIDUALITY

"The creatures that inhabit this
earth—be they human beings or
animals—are here to contribute, each
in its own particular way, to the beauty
and prosperity of the world."

—14th Dalai Lama

Power Your Life WITH FAITH IN YOURSELF

"It's a lack of faith that makes people
afraid of meeting challenges, and I
believe in myself."

—Muhammad Ali

PROFILE #39:
USE LIFE'S LESSONS TO KEEP GROWING

Actor and Producer Isaiah Washington

"Time and tide wait for no man." Whether we recognize it or not, each one of us is heading towards something. That "something" can be the fulfillment of a dream—or, if we choose to be apathetic, the result of our slackness will be failure. No matter what position we hold or what we assume about ourselves, there is a journey we are on that will take us wherever we want to go. The question becomes this: Will you be a better individual because of it?

I'm not a huge television person, and though I knew that actor Isaiah Washington had been on the hit TV series *Grey's Anatomy* and starred in several movies, I wasn't that familiar with him and his body of work—until 2011, that is. Late in that year, I saw a write-up about his book, *A Man from Another Land: How Finding My Roots Changed My Life*.

Isaiah Washington showed me the power of our individual platforms, and I think will demonstrate it for you as well. He knows what it's like to succeed and to face challenges, but he is not one to quit. We've had the pleasure of enjoying a few conversations over the years, the first of which happened when he was preparing for the release of his project *Blue Caprice* at the Sundance Film Festival.

So how does Mr. Washington feel about the love his fans around the world continually have for him? "I'm still humbled by it and pleasantly surprised," he told me. "I'm still learning how fans are in the television world. It's a powerful connection they develop with you. They don't let you go."

The gift that is his ability to bring characters to life and draw you in as a viewer in the process is something he realized through a mentor early in his career. "He said to me, 'If you knew what you had you would mess it up.'"

"I never really knew I had this gift until I started to have this dream about it."

Whatever brought about his dream of sharing his gift with the world, it proved to Isaiah that he could make this happen for himself—and that is exactly what he did.

Speaking to a man who is ever the professional, but someone who knows what it's like to be in the spotlight and to have all eyes on him, I was curious as to how he kept the glare of celebrity from blinding him. His answer was real, and more than I could have imagined he would share. "I made a huge mistake and forgot my place in the world and forgot that the world was looking at me and that I had this particular power and gift," he said, referencing the incident that occurred at the 2007 Golden Globes. "I was only thinking about myself in that moment. When you are in pain and in trauma, you respond. ... In hindsight I realize that if I knew the power I had when I was on that hit show, then things would have been amazingly different—but I wouldn't be able to have this conversation with you now."

That to me was a profound statement for him to make, but I think it is a great reminder for all of us. Bad things might be the doorway to the unbelievable blessings that are meant to be a part of your journey.

"Unfortunately for me in my ignorance," Washington continued, "I refused to accept my position as a role model. I know now that was a mistake."

"Anyone who is afforded to live the lifestyle I have lived has the responsibility to share that. You always have to be cognizant of how you show up."

"Now I am aligned with that."

This revelation that Isaiah Washington has had, however, is not an excuse for us to forget that he is still just a man. "I believe this is true for all of us," he says. "It is the understanding of how to play your position at any given moment in time. It's important to know that I'm a human being just like you, but I never want to lose sight of that part of my humanity. As long as you remain humble and connected to the idea that each of us are what I call 'perfect imperfection,' I can continue to do the things I say I want to do and leave a legacy that my family and friends can be proud of."

The biggest lesson for us is that you don't have to be a celebrity to have this type of epiphany about yourself and who you are in the world.

"I have been given an extraordinary privilege," *Washington told me, "but we all have been given a* *gift. We have to understand that each and every one* *of us has a divine purpose."*

1. If you have made a wrong step, how can Isaiah's example encourage you to keep going?

2. Though it seems as though the switch to your positivity might be off, what can you do today to turn it back on and bring the power back?

Power Your Life WITH SELF-FORGIVENESS

"Freedom is not worth having if it does not connote freedom to err."

—Ghandi

Power Your Life BY BEING A MENTOR

"You are where you are today because you stand on somebody's shoulders. And wherever you are heading, you cannot get there by yourself. If you stand on the shoulders of others, you have a reciprocal responsibility to live your life so that others may stand on your shoulders. It's the quid pro quo of life. We exist temporarily through what we take, but we live forever through what we give."

—Vernon Jordan

Power Your Life WITH GRATITUDE FOR LIFE

"When you arise in the morning, think of what a precious privilege it is to be alive —to breathe, to think, to enjoy, to love."

—Marcus Aurelius

Power Your Life BY FORGIVING MISTAKES

"To judge a man by his weakest link or deed is like judging the power of the ocean by one wave."

—Elvis Presley

PROFILE #40:
THE BEST IS YET TO COME

Actor Sam Humphrey

He might be the last profile in this book, but actor Sam Humphrey has proven to be one of my favorite conversations I'm sharing with you. He has had his share of challenges and difficulties, but he wouldn't give up and is winning big time. In 2017, we saw him make his debut in his first feature film which happens to be one of the biggest movies of the year: *The Greatest Showman*.

I've interviewed several cast members from *The Greatest Showman* now, but Sam was the first I interviewed—and he showcased both his talent and the importance of keeping a positive attitude about life, no matter what.

For those who haven't seen *The Greatest Showman*, all I can say is that it's one of the most inspiring films I have seen in some time. Sam and I discussed the film, his pursuit of his dreams, and his vision of what he hopes you realize is possible for you.

"It's been a really amazing and positive experience,"
he told me, discussing the success of the movie. "Just
seeing all the reactions from the public, it's just been
overwhelming." I asked him when they were filming it if
they knew it was something special at the time. He told
me they hoped that the film's "message of acceptance
and that anything is possible" was something that the
cast hoped the public would rally around. "Also the idea
that you can decide your own destiny."

It was at the age of eight that Sam knew acting was
something he wanted to do, and the person that
inspired him in that direction is the person he is now
starring with in this amazing film: Hugh Jackman. "He's
been the best teacher that I could possibly have," Sam
told me. "It's a very surreal thing, to go from wanting it
as a kid and only dreaming of attaining it to now being
an actor that's succeeding." And it's something he
doesn't take for granted.

Having had challenges growing up has helped Sam
keep the right perspective about life and especially
fear. "It's sort of something that I've wanted to do,"
he says when it comes to acting.

> *"With the challenges I've gone through, I told myself that if I went through that, nothing could stop me from whatever I wanted to do in life."*

He also says having positive mentors and a great support system have kept him from giving into fear.

> *His message to you: "We all get sidetracked. We get hung up on things that aren't really important. The important thing is to get back aligned with what really matters and follow your dreams no matter what."*

1. How can you get realigned to your goals and dreams after being sidetracked?

2. In spite of challenges why are your goals worth pursuing?

Power Your Life BY TAKING BABY STEPS

"Step by step walk the thousand-mile road."

—Miyamoto Musashi

Power Your Life WITH CHEERFULNESS

"Let us go singing as far as we go:
the road will be less tedious."

—Virgil

Power Your Life BY WEATHERING THE STORM

"Endure, and keep yourselves for days
of happiness."

—Virgil

**Power Your Life BY LOOKING
FOR A WAY TO HELP**

"Believe, when you are most unhappy,
that there is something for you to do in
the world. So long as you can sweeten
another's pain, life is not in vain."

—Helen Keller

AFTERWORD

When people ask me how I am able to stay so motived and focused on my goals and vision, one of the main ways is by what you hold in your hands right now. This book is more than about celebrities and their stories. It's about all of us being connected and capable of achieving amazing things—if we realize that it's part of our makeup to want to win.

I hope that this book inspires you to look for ways you can power up your life and choose a more positive direction that can help not just you but prove to be an example for others. It doesn't matter what you want in your life. The important thing is to not stop striving until you attain it.

I would love to hear your thoughts about those profiled in this book. Feel free to reach out to me at cawebb4@juno.com and follow me on social media at the links below. We're in this thing called life together. Let's do our part to encourage one another.

Cyrus Webb

ACKNOWLEDGMENTS

This book would not have been made possible without the relationships I have formed with the individuals featured here. Thanks for trusting me with your stories and your time—and for being an example for us all of what you can do when you choose to power your life with the positive instead of the alternative.

For the supporters of *Conversations LIVE* the radio show, *Conversations Magazine*, and *Cyrus Webb Presents* the web series, thanks for allowing the conversations I've shared with you to not just entertain but inspire you over the years. My success in these endeavors would not have been possible without you.

And to you, the readers of this book, may you be able to realize that what you want is possible and attainable if you are willing to believe and do the work.

ABOUT THE AUTHOR

Cyrus Webb is a radio and TV personality, artist, author, and poet who has built a brand based on the power of words and expression.

He is a Mississippi native and hosts *Conversations LIVE*, a radio show that has over one million listeners around the world and is heard on the radio dial in Mississippi as well as through several online outlets such as iHeartRadio. He is the founder as well as Editor-In-Chief of *Conversations Magazine* as well as the founder of Conversations Book Club, the south's largest co-ed book club that has hosted over three hundred authors since 2007.

In 2018 he was recognized by *Brotha Magazine* as one of their Men of the Year, and he has been one of Amazon.com's Top Influencers since 2014. Webb's mission is to inspire and motivate individuals to realize their potential and pursue their goals and dreams.

Stay connected with Webb at:

www.cyruswebb.com
www.facebook.com/cyruswebb
www.twitter.com/cyruswebb
www.instagram.com/cyruswebbpresents